The Herbal Kitchen

The Herbal Kitchen

By Dan and Myrl Moran

Adventure Publications
Cambridge, Minnesota

Published by:
Adventure Publications, Inc.
P.O. Box 269
Cambridge, MN 55008
1-800-678-7006

Printed in the United States of America.
ISBN 1-885061-12-9

Cover and interior design by Paula Roth.
Cover and interior illustrations by Julie Janke.
Edited by Derek J. Anderson.

TABLE OF CONTENTS

'Herb (urb, hurb) n...
1. a seed plant
which does not develop
woody persistent tissue
(as that of a shrub or a tree),
but is more or less
soft and succulent;
specially, one used for
medicinal purposes,
or for its sweet scent
or flavor...."

Introduction

Herbal Kitchen is actually two books in one. On the one hand it is a book on growing herbs, offering tips on the propagation, planting, growing, harvesting, and preserving of herbs in your own home or garden. On the other hand, it is a cookbook, offering tips on the use of herbs, including recipes for everything from soups to main courses to herbal teas.

This book is, we believe, the best of both worlds. Culled from the Moran's many years of growing and using herbs on their organic herb farm (The Melon Patch, in rural Minnesota) it offers a great introduction to the world of herb growing—told with humor, wit, and, most importantly, experience.

We've formatted this book to be as "user friendly" as possible, starting out with practical general advice on how to grow, propagate, and preserve herbs. The rest of the book includes specific discussions of individual herbs. These chapters are presented with a basic introduction, then a look at the propagation, growing, harvesting, preserving, and cooking nuances of that specific herb.

In this book, the Morans share their many years of first-hand experience with herbs, most of which has been acquired in the Upper Midwest. Keep this in mind while reading about the guidelines for growing seasons, winter protection, etc. You'll want to check zone charts for your area for specific frost dates. The zones referred to in the book are the United States Department of Agriculture growing zones. They are based on minimum temperatures for the area. So, in zone 3, the winter temperatures would not generally fall below -40°F. The Morans farm close to the northern edge of zone 4, and zone 3 is north of them. While all the herbs may be grown almost anywhere in the US and Canada, some guidelines for winter protection and mulching, for example, may not apply in all areas. Also, in a warmer climate, you may be able to plant and harvest "winter" crops.

What are Herbs?

'Herb (urb,hurb) n... 1. a seed plant which does not develop woody persistent tissue (as that of a shrub or a tree), but is more or less soft and succulent; specially, one used for medicinal purposes, or for its sweet scent or flavor...."

"Herb" is a word that seems to stir up pleasant sensations in the human brain. It may be a memory of Grandma's kitchen, with bunches of thyme drying behind the wood range, or a special herbal medicine that Mother used for colds. For some people it might be the wonderful smell of sweet basil on a sunny day, or perhaps a unique herbal tea in that quaint little shop. The words "herb" and "spice" are often used interchangeably, but a rule of thumb is herbs are green and spices brown. Herbs, in general, are found in more temperate climates, while spices are more tropical.

For the purposes of this book we've loosely defined an herb as any plant used for seasoning foods, or for its fragrance. We think herbs are charming and exciting plants to study, grow, and use. We want to share with you the experiences we have had growing herbs, and provide instructions for growing and using some of the more popular herbs.

We first started growing herbs many years ago with just a few—parsley, chives, and rosemary. As we learned and experimented, we expanded our selection of herbs until we were growing over 160 varieties! Growing herbs is now our full-time occupation. We sell the majority of our crop to a local farmers market. We both really love what we do, and while it is our livelihood, we are not that concerned with making a lot of money. We try hard not to pollute this wonderful land that we are borrowing for a little while, and at the same time we try to get along with our fellow human beings.

Cooking with Herbs

Cooking with herbs is a sure way to take pleasure in life. Whether you chop up robust green basil for a hearty pesto bread, add a generous sprig of rosemary to your roasting chicken, or make a delicious thyme-and-garlic marinade for a meat dish, you can use herbs to add wonderful smells and tastes to your kitchen. Cooking with herbs is not difficult. It can be as simple as garnishing a dish with a fresh sprig of the same herb used to flavor it. Try, for example, snipping a handful of chervil onto your delicate chervil soup!

Herbs mean more than taste; herbs are healthy. Concerned about salt in your diet? Season with herbs instead! Herbs contain few calories, so enjoy large amounts with each meal—for their flavors, vitamins, and medicinal value. Herbs have been used for health and pleasure for thousands of years. For example, a little mint, basil, or ginger adds taste to a meal and has a carminative effect, soothing and settling the digestive tract. A little savory or epazote added to a bean dish will have the same effect. In sushi bars, ginger slices are served as a carminative and a palate clearer. Last but not least, a handful of chopped, curled parsley is a good idea in garlic dishes; it helps prevent garlic breath.

Home-grown herbs add zest and variety to your dishes. Consider what you can do with garnishes. Cinnamon basil has a gorgeous, purplish blossom that adds a nice touch. The lavender flowers of onion chives, the white blossoms of garlic chives—and the leaves of both—look and taste good on almost anything. The ubiquitous Johnny jump-up (viola) is lovely and edible. Try the purple basils: purple ruffles, dark opal, or red holy. Both kinds of parsley, curled and Italian, are delicious both as garnishes and as an essential flavor in a dish.

When cooking with herbs, enjoy the visual presentation. Drop lemon balm leaves into your finger bowls, or add a large sprig of mint to each glass of iced tea! Lay a fresh branch of flowers on the napkins, and get out those pretty blue dishes!

Try to include herbs of different textures: the ferny fronds of baby dill, the more crisp basil, the firm bits of minced rosemary, and the coarse bay leaves. Different colors add as much to dishes as different textures. We love to tuck a branch of purple ruffles basil into a salad. Deep-colored basil is also a beautiful treat when snipped with French tarragon onto a bowl of melon balls.

The Japanese certainly know the importance of visual presentation in cooking. Myrl especially remembers the way a wonderful lunch of *kaiseki*, the finest of the traditional Japanese cuisine, was served. She was the guest of her friend Hiroe.

There were several courses and each contained many dishes— perhaps fifty. Each course was graciously served by a different kimono-clad woman who knelt by the table to uncover and arrange the sumptuous array. The food was accented with natural beauty: chrysanthemum leaves, plum blossoms, maple leaves, and mats made from twigs. The exquisite dishes were small, usually covered, in shades of blue and orange; hot dishes, cold dishes—even an edible dish made of dried baby fish.

Fresh herbs were served in tiny dishes, perhaps only 1 inch in diameter. The herbs were picked up with chopsticks and dipped into another small bowl containing a special sauce. Then bits of fish were dipped into this mouth-watering combination and eaten.

Hiroe, kneeling on her pillow and back straight as an arrow, would gaze intently at the lovely dishes as the server moved them from a wooden box and placed them on the low table. For perhaps a full minute she would drink in the beauty of the food, the colors, textures, and fragrances. Then she would smile, and pick up her chopsticks. The entire meal was a study in pleasure—and much of it stemmed from the visual presentation of each dish.

You will be surprised at how quickly you can make visual presentation a wonderful part of your cooking. Let your imagination go. Bring out that bright Mexican serape for a tablecloth! Set the table with a variety of dishes! Don't be afraid to use Aunt Ella's deep orange covered bowl, and dust off that Shaker platter! Using herbs, try dressing up your table with dozens of Johnny jump-up blossoms, freshly picked and dried on a towel for a few minutes. You can pick the flowers several hours ahead of time, and wash and refrigerate them. About an hour before your guests arrive, scatter the little beauties down the center of the table and on the napkins, or use them with deep orange nasturtium blossoms to garnish your salad.

Cooking with herbs emphasizes presentation. The sensual pleasure of an appealing meal feeds both the spirit and the imagination. The taste, smell, and beauty of food do as much for our spirits as they do for our bodies.

Fragrance is also important to an appealing dish, and herbs are certainly fragrant. There is the clean, deep aroma of lemon verbena, the heady whiff of Hawaii coming from pineapple sage, the strong evergreen of rosemary, and the almost musky richness of oregano. Remember Grandma's sage dressing on Thanksgiving or the oregano-basil aroma of pizza, fresh from the oven? Imagine the scent of a large sprig of spearmint floating on iced tea swirling in a tall frosted glass. Our sense of smell is reputed to be thousands of times more sensitive than taste, so it makes sense to increase the anticipation of a great meal with the wafting nuances of herbs.

By growing fresh herbs, you not only know exactly how your herbs were grown, but you also gain the delightful pleasure of gardening. Imagine yourself gathering a large handful of basil leaves on a sunny morning. You wash them gently, shake off the excess water, and arrange the fresh basil on a large platter. Next, you cover the platter with slices of your delicious tomatoes, add just a touch of oil and vinegar plus a garnish of basil blossoms, and *Bellissima!*

Do we overstate our case when we say herbs are truly wonderful? We think not. Consider the joys of working in the sun to produce your own food. Then you can relish gathering your herbs. Snipping warm, full-bodied basil leaves while the rich aroma tantalizes you, or caressing sage leaves to release their scent and flavor—these are some of life's simple pleasures. Preparing food using herbs is certainly rewarding. As you chop garlic, mince rosemary, steep lemon verbena for tea, or stir your lovage soup, your kitchen is filled with warmth, life, and joy.

Of course, the ultimate pleasure in herb cooking is the eating. Just imagine the tasty licorice of French tarragon on your broiled pike, the marriage of onion and sage in your dressing, or the walnutty touch of arugula in your Bibb lettuce salad.

Herbs help you get the taste you like. The quality and strength of an herb's flavor, both fresh and dried, vary greatly depending on when, and how, it is harvested and stored. We offer measurements in our recipes, but we suggest that you taste as you go in cooking. After all, that's half the fun! Welcome to the happiness of herbs. We are sure you will enjoy cooking with herbs.

CHAPTER 1

General Tips for Growing Herbs

The only way to get started growing herbs is to start. You will find herb gardening an enjoyable, relaxing hobby. There is just something about an herb garden on a sunny day that adds a lot to life. Your herb garden can comprise anything from a pot of parsley on your kitchen window sill to a hundred acres of mint grown for its essential oils. Growing herbs is so easy that anyone can do it.

If you are an absolute beginner to gardening, we suggest that you start with just a few plants. Those that grow quickly, like basil, chives, and mint, are good choices. We also suggest that you start with plants, good strong ones, in a 4-inch pots (for northern gardeners), rather than starting your herbs from seed. That way, with a strong start, you will be enjoying your herbs weeks earlier than if you had seeded them.

Find a location in full sun (except as indicated for specific herbs), and a little wind protection. Since herbs are quite forgiving, you don't need great soil, but it should be well-drained. Work the soil up well, work in some plant food, transplant your herbs, and water them when dry.

Whether you start with a 1- by 5-foot box outside your kitchen door or plunge into growing herbs on a large scale for the restaurants in your town, we guarantee that you will find great rewards working with these lovely-smelling and good-tasting plants.

Starting

You can start your herbs either by buying them in a nursery, seeding them, or by vegetative propagation from an existing plant.

If you buy your herb plants instead of growing them from seed, we recommend that you purchase plants in at least the 4-inch size container. This will give you a well started plant with the necessary well-developed root system. The plant should be a healthy color, with no yellowing around the edges of the leaves or on the bottom leaves.

The plant should not be root bound. To look for this, tip the pot to one side and gently ease the plant an inch or so out of the pot. If the roots go round and round the rootball and are discolored, the seedling is too old, and will take a long time to get going in your garden.

An important thing to remember is that the plants have just come from the protected environment of a greenhouse. Therefore, they should not be placed in a cold, windy outdoor environment until they have adjusted to the situation. This is called "hardening off" and is just a gradual conditioning of the plant to the outside—a few hours, then half a day, etc.

Seeding can be accomplished directly in the garden, or by starting seeds indoors in flats. Ninety-nine percent of our herbs are started in seed flats and then transplanted into larger containers. At that point we either sell them in the containers or transplant them into our gardens to grow and sell as cut herbs. We seed the remaining one percent directly into our gardens. Some herbs do not tolerate transplanting well, so refer to the individual plant entries for specific information.

There are three main advantages to starting the plants indoors. First, we can better control the temperature, soil moisture, and light. Second, the additional step of thinning or blocking directly-seeded plants is eliminated, and third, we can begin outdoor weed control in the fields before we have plants to work around.

There are three main methods of vegetative propagation: division, rooting, and layering. Division is a propagation method used with plants such as French tarragon and goldenseal that have clearly-defined crowns. Each crown is actually a stem that is growing from the roots.

To divide a plant either in the spring or fall you dig up the entire plant with all of its root system. Wash the soil from the root mass with a hose and the individual crowns will then be obvious.

With some herbs, such as valerian, you can gently pull off each crown with its attached root. French tarragon, however, has to be cut apart with a sharp knife. Not all herbs can be propagated by division. We divide French tarragon, goldenseal, and valerian.

Rooting involves the growing of new roots on a piece of stem cut from an herb that you wish to propagate. This is the same method many of you have used when you have taken a piece of a houseplant and put it in a glass of water to grow new roots. This technique will work with some herbs, such as the basils, mints, and some sages.

Cut a 2- to 3-inch section of the tip of a stem. Remove all of the leaves from the lower half of the stem and place it tip end up in a container filled with a wet Cornell Peat-Lite mix, page 12, fortified with extra calcium sulfate, 2 tablespoons per cubic foot, to stimulate rooting. Make a dome over the container with a clear plastic sack held in place with a rubber band. Place the container in a warm, light environment out of the direct sunlight until small roots form. Depending on the type of herb that you are rooting, root formation should take place between one week (mint) and six months (laurel).

Layering is a method of vegetative propagation by which you lay a living branch or stem on soil and pin it down until roots form where it touches the soil. Then you remove the branch from the parent plant and transplant it. This method can be used for herbs that sprawl and creep on the ground, such as thyme, rosemary, sage, and oregano.

Because herbs comprise such a diverse group of plants, it is difficult to generalize too much about their growing habits. Some germinate readily, others germinate well but take a long time to break the soil, and some germinate so poorly that much restraint is needed to wait them out. Below are general guidelines that we think apply to most herbs. We have included specific growing hints in our discussions of the individual herbs in following chapters.

Seeding in Trays

For herbs that we start from seed, we sow the seeds in plastic cell trays. They are like the four-packs or six-packs you buy your bedding plants in, except that all the cells are connected. We usually use trays measuring 10- by 20-inches that have 50 or 72 cells each. We use the trays over and over, but we sterilize them between plantings with household laundry bleach—one part bleach to nine parts water. We first clean the trays of any leftover soil or plant-growing medium using a stiff brush and hot soapsuds. Next, we dunk them for 2 minutes in the bleach solution, and let them air dry for an hour. We work quickly, as the chlorine vapors kill plants. Obviously, then, we don't do our sterilizing in the greenhouse, and we are careful to use an area with good ventilation, so the chlorine vapors don't also kill us!

We fill the sterilized trays with a soil mix called "Cornell", which is similar to most commercial soil mixes.

❧ *Cornell Soil Mix* ❧
(Cornell Peat-Lite Mix)

½ cubic yard sphagnum peat moss
½ cubic yard horticultural vermiculite
10 pounds ground dolomite
5 pounds steamed bone meal (organic phosphate)
1 pound calcium nitrate or potassium nitrate

Because such a mix is nearly sterile to begin with, most damping-off problems are eliminated. (Damping-off is the technical term for the rotting of the little seedlings just as they emerge, caused by a variety of soil-borne fungi.) An advantage of the soil mix is that because it is a light, airy mixture, you will not run as high a risk of over-watering, which can be a major problem indoors. But the down-side of using soil mixes is that if they are allowed to dry out, it is difficult to get them wet again. The mixes are also popular with fungus gnats. These pesky pests are not a huge problem, but if they get out of hand, they can cause root problems. We control them through good sanitation, keeping all trash off the greenhouse floor where they breed. Flytraps will catch some of the adults.

After we fill the trays with the seed-starting medium, we wet them thoroughly and let the trays drain for a day. Then we seed the trays through a method known as drilling. A drilled row is a single straight row fed out of the fist. A wide row is comprised of several rows that are close together.

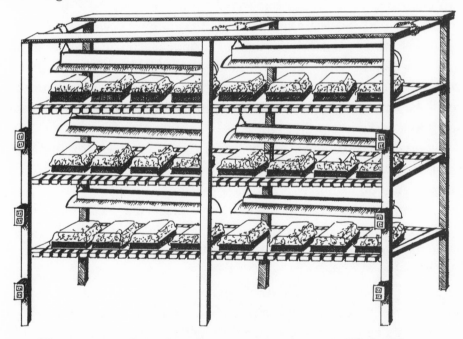

The trays are then placed in a germination unit. We build our own germination units, each consisting of three shelves with a Ken-Bar thermostatically-controlled heating pad on the floor of each shelf and eight 40-watt cool white fluorescent tubes on the ceiling of each shelf. We keep the units in our basement, which averages 55°F in late winter. The heating pads keep the soil temperature between 55 and 95°F, wherever we set the thermostat. In general, most herbs will germinate at 70-75°F, but there are many exceptions. Basils, for example, germinate faster (and better) at 85-90°F, while English lavender germinates best at 55°F.

To conserve heat we cover the units with white plastic until later in the season when the basement temperature rises. We also set a fan beside the unit to keep air moving across it.

We suggest that you have at least a four-foot shelf light of two fluorescent tubes because it is difficult to get enough light to grow plants indoors. Install the light where it can be on 14 to 16 hours a day, and arrange it so you can water the seed containers.

Seeding

Many herb seeds are small to insignificant in size, while others are very large. Some seeds require light to germinate, so you plant them on the surface of the soil. Others germinate in the dark, so they should be covered with soil. The depth to cover them depends on the size of the seed, the larger the seed the deeper you plant it. Generally, you plant seeds to a depth 2 to 3 times their size.

Some herb seeds will need a cold treatment called stratification prior to planting. This applies to herbs that generally grow in a cold climate. A good example in *Echinacea purpurea.*

A simple stratification method is to place the seeds in a small container of damp sand or other damp material, such as perlite, and place the container in your refrigerator. We use small, clear plastic bags closed with a twist-tie.

The period of time in the refrigerator will vary by species, so you should consult a germination chart. Most seed houses will inform you in their catalog or on the package as to whether or not the seed needs stratification, the length of time to stratify, and whether or not the seed needs light to germinate.

Whether you are germinating your herbs on a kitchen window sill or in a germination unit in your basement, most of them need light to germinate. In order to keep your plants from "stretching", getting wimpy and lanky, we recommend a 16-hour light day. If you are using fluorescent lights, keep them about 3 inches above the seedlings.

More plants are killed by overwatering than any other cause. The seeds require moisture to germinate and live, but they also need oxygen in the soil to grow. Too much water replaces the oxygen, so you do not want the soil soggy.

We recommend that you wait until the soil is dry to the touch. Then water thoroughly, so the water runs out the bottom of the container. The time it takes a plant to dry out depends on all of the variables: type of soil, how warm it is, size of container, etc.

Field Soil Preparation

For annuals, we prepare the field to receive the young plants 4 to 5 weeks before transplanting. We plow, disk, and harrow the soil, just like farmers do for corn and wheat. After the first flush of weeds are up, we give the area a shallow cultivation of 2 to 3 inches with a disk or spike-tooth harrow, to prevent stirring up any more dormant weed seeds than absolutely necessary. Then, depending on the weed population, heat, and moisture, we give the soil one or two more shallow cultivations. We transplant our plants immediately after the final cultivation.

When you are figuring out just how close together to place your herb plants in the ground, you should consider the size that the mature plant will be, the necessity to cultivate between plants, and the aesthetic appearance that you wish to achieve.

After transplanting, one more shallow cultivation is likely to last the whole season, unless we have some pesky perennial weeds (e.g. quack grass), or annuals (e.g. wild proso millet), that germinate deeper in the soil.

Fertilization

It is difficult to generalize on fertilization, since so much depends on your soil's natural nutrient level. It has been our experience that most of the herbs we grow do best in a well-fertilized situation. In the organic tradition we use compost and manure that we get from a neighbor's dairy farm. (Of course the manure does introduce some weed seeds, but we figure that weeds are a given anyway.) We think that if you have a nice loamy soil and add a couple of inches of compost per year, you will need little or no added fertilizer.

Ph Balance

We try to keep our naturally acidic soil at a ph of 6.5, but it is not an easy task. A ph of 7 is neutral, under 7 is acid, battery acid is about 3.5, and over 7 is alkaline. A strong lye solution measures about ph 9 or 10.

We alter the ph of our soil by spreading agricultural dolomitic lime (ground limestone). "Dolomitic" means it contains magnesium as well as calcium, nutrients that the soil needs. To move the ph of our sandy soil up one unit, from 5.5 to 6.5 for instance, we spread two pounds of dolomitic lime per 100 square feet. Most of the plants we are discussing do quite well in a slightly acidic soil.

If your soil is alkaline it can be treated with elemental sulphur, which reacts with the alkaline soil to move the ph toward the acidic end. For methods, see your fertilizer dealer or County Extension agent.

Irrigation

Our soil is very well drained, and we irrigate weekly during the hot, dry summer weeks. When temperatures average about 70°F with some wind, we try to put on 2 inches of water a week, including rainfall. If the temperature averages 65°F, we shoot for 1½ inches, and at 60°F and below, about 1 inch.

Mulching for Winter

If plants are of doubtful hardiness, it is a good idea to mulch them. Wait until the ground freezes, then lay evergreen branches over the plants. Next, cover everything with 4 to 6 inches of clean fluffed straw. If there is a chance that the wind might blow the straw away, weight it down with more evergreen boughs, or anything else that will hold it.

In the spring, wait until early grasses and sprouts start to sprout, then remove the mulch over a 4 or 5 day period. Don't pull it all off suddenly, but uncover a little bit of the plant each day for a week. Watch out for hard frosts, and cover the plants again if frost is forecast. The plants under the mulch will already be starting to grow, so you don't want to subject them to either full sun or a raging storm all at once.

Gardening by Zen

Gardening is still much more of an art than a science. If you don't believe it, go to a fertilizer dealer or agricultural college to have your soil sampled. Then, do everything that is recommended for soil and foliar fertilization, pest control, drainage, herbicides, plastic mulches, row covers, anti-desiccants, etc. See how the scientist scores against you, the artist. Our society has become so impressed with technology that it is tempting to use it even when it does not fit in the hole. (And that is where we will end up if we try to follow every scientific recommendation—in the hole!)

Plants are much like us—they need room to grow, not too much competition, a little water, some sunlight and food, maybe a little sex and nurturing, and they'll get along just fine.

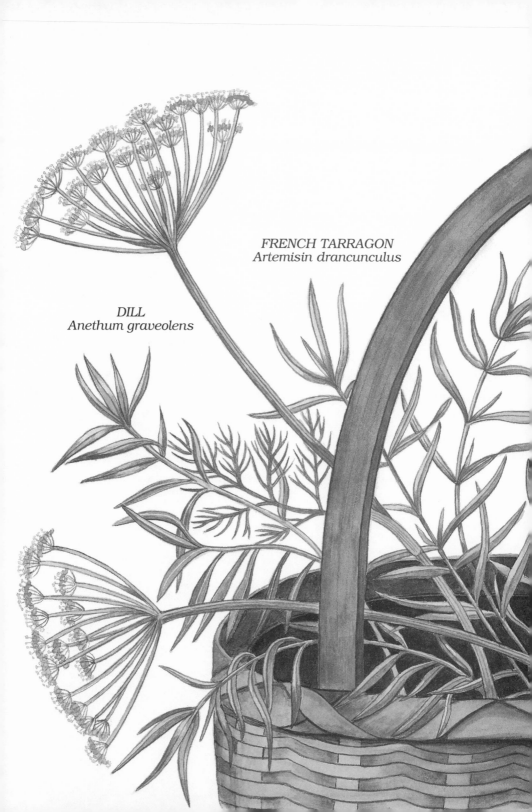

FRENCH TARRAGON
Artemisin drancunculus

DILL
Anethum graveolens

Harvesting and Preserving Your Herbs

So you've labored lovingly all summer over your prize garden, filled with fragrant, eye-catching, and tasty herbs. When fall comes, it's time to preserve some of their beauty. Perhaps you will hang bunches of drying herbs in your kitchen, some to rub, some to jar, and others just to have hanging for their aroma and appearance. Perhaps you and your grandchild will make tiny baskets filled with rose hips for the holiday tree, or maybe you will use your herbs in sachets and soaps!

You can dry herbs, freeze them, make vinegars and syrups, or butters and pesto. The seeds can be dried and stored for cooking. Potpourri is a popular way to preserve these aromatic plants, as are bouquets or wreaths. Whichever preservation method you choose will allow you to hang on to that wonderful herbal summer.

Drying Herbs

To dry herbs, pick the best leaves and branches on a clear summer morning after the dew has gone, since that is the time when their fragrant oil content is the highest. For drying herb flowers, you will want to pick the blossoms when they have just opened.

To dry herbs in bunches, gently wash any dust from them. Hang them in small bunches upside-down, out of direct sunlight, in a well-ventilated room. If you want, you may put a small bag over each bunch to keep the dust off. Four herbs that are easy to hang-dry are sage, thyme, oregano, and sweet marjoram.

Maybe building a drying rack would be a good family project. Some are made simply of dowels glued into a frame. A collapsible towel rack is also good for drying herbs. You can also lay the herbs out to dry on a screen borrowed from a window. It will take about 2 weeks for hanging herbs to dry completely.

You can speed up the process by placing the herbs on a rack in a 100°F oven, door ajar, for 3 to 4 hours. A microwave oven may also be used. It takes from 1 to 3 minutes on a medium setting, but the leaves must be turned every 30 seconds.

Whichever drying method you use, be sure the herbs are totally dry or else they will mold in storage. Once dry, the herbs can be rubbed between your hands onto a clean towel. Discard the stems and store the rubbed leaves in an air-tight jar out of direct sunlight. Leaves for tea are best if they are kept as whole as possible. Remember, if you are cooking with dried herbs, the formula, at least to start with, is ½ teaspoon dried herbs = 2 scant teaspoon fresh herbs.

Freezing

Freezing herbs is really simple, and the flavors stay good for several months. Some herbs will discolor, but they still hold their flavor. To freeze, just gently wash and pat dry. Do not blanch. Put the herbs into small bags, label, and freeze. The frozen herbs are fragile, so don't stack anything on top of them. We freeze parsley, basil, chervil, dill, marjoram, and lemon thyme. Use the same amount of frozen herbs in recipes as you would use fresh.

Freezing in Oil

Freezing herbs in oil is also a popular way to preserve your summer harvest. The ratio of herb to oil is 2 cups of fresh herb to ⅓ to ½ cup of oil. While you can use any oil that you would use for cooking, we use canola oil.

Finely chop the herbs in a food processor or blender, gradually adding the oil until the mix reaches the consistency of peanut butter. Freeze the mixture in a small container.

For use, scrape off a small amount as needed. Use the same amount of frozen herb oil as you would fresh herb in your recipe. For example, if a recipe calls for 1 tablespoon fresh chopped basil, you could substitute 1 tablespoon frozen basil in oil.

We have frozen basil, oregano, and rosemary in oil, but you may try others. You can also blend herbs in a mixture to be frozen. The herb to oil ratio remains the same. A delicious example of this would be garlic with basil.

As we understand it, the reason for freezing your herb/oil mixture is because botulism spores can grow in an airless environment if left at room temperature (or even in the refrigerator)!

Herb Butter

Herb butters are another way to enhance your culinary creations. You can use individual herbs, such as dill, or combinations, such as garlic and basil.

The ratio we use is ¼ pound softened butter to two tablespoons chopped fresh herbs. Of course, you can modify this to your taste. Once the fresh herbs are finely chopped, cream them into the softened butter. Give the process a few hours to meld the flavors before you serve it.

Herb butter can either be shaped with a butter mold or rolled into a cylinder shape for serving. It can be refrigerated for a few days, or frozen for 2 or 3 months. If you plan to freeze it, wrap the cylinder in waxed paper and then aluminum foil. Then, once it is frozen, it is a simple matter to open the package and slice off pats as you want them.

It's wonderful what tarragon/garlic butter will do for a walleye fillet, and herb butters are also good for baked potatoes, sweet corn, vegetables, chops, steaks, egg dishes, and broiled or poached fish fillets.

Herb Vinegar

Herb vinegars are wonderful on salads, in sauces, and in any recipe that calls for vinegar. We suggest making vinegars from French tarragon, chives, dark opal or purple ruffles basil, or oregano. For each bottle of vinegar use 1 cup crushed herb leaves (or more if you prefer), and 2 cups of vinegar. Pick the green leaves of the herb just before flowering (except for oregano–pick that when it flowers). Wash and dry the leaves. Crush the herbs or cut them into small pieces. Put into a large jar and cover with the vinegar. Let stand out of sunlight for 2 to 4 weeks. Strain and bottle the liquid in clean bottles, with air-tight plastic caps, or corks sealed with wax. (The reason to avoid metallic caps is that vinegar is acidic, and the metal will react with vinegar.) If you like, put in a fresh sprig of the herb you vinegared into the bottle. Lovely chive blossoms and deep purple basil leaves are absolutely beautiful in vinegar. Herb vinegars last 1 or 2 years, depending on how much you dilute the original vinegar's acidity.

Herb Syrups

Put 1 cup clean herb leaves and flowers (try lemon verbena or mint) into a heat-proof glass bowl. Add 1½ cups boiling water, cover, and leave for 3 hours. Strain. Add 1 cup sugar for each 1½ cups liquid. Cook over medium heat until the sugar dissolves. Then cook 3 minutes more. Cool and jar. Herb syrups are used as flavorings for drinks, liqueurs, fresh fruits, and toppings for ice cream, yogurt, and pudding.

Potpourri

This lovely concoction of dried herbs and flower petals is easy to make, and it will give your home a lovely smell as it either sits in a pretty bowl or simmers in a little water on the stove.

The ingredients are up to you. We usually start with petals–those of the wild rose are wonderful, and you can add some rose hips for color. Cinnamon basil flowers have an excellent basil smell, they have good color, and they are firm. Experiment with petals from any of your flowers. Try adding scented geranium leaves, thymes, mint, basil, lemon verbena, or rosemary. It's best to mix up several different potpourris and see, or smell, which one you like best.

Basic Potpourri

3 cups dried flower petals and herbs

3 cinnamon sticks

cloves and ginger (Add 1 tablespoon to start with and more if you think it needs it)

1 tablespoon orris root per quart of herbs or flowers (orris root acts as a fixative but other fixatives are rosemary, rose scented geraniums, and *horsemint Monarda punctata.*)

Stir everything together, and store in air-tight jars. Potpourri makes a lovely gift, especially tied with a ribbon and hand-labeled card.

Tussie Mussie

For a hand-held herbal bouquet to put to your nose as needed to help cover any unpleasant smell, try making a Tussie Mussie. Start with a center flower—a rose, some lavender blossoms or a few nasturtiums. Circle the flower with a green herb, perhaps sage, and tie with yarn. Add another circle of scented geraniums. Tie. Next add a circle of Lavender leaves and blossoms. Encircle the whole Tussie Mussie with a paper doily, add pretty ribbon, and you've got it!

Hair Rinses

Rosemary and chamomile can be preserved in hair rinses. To brighten dark hair, put a handful of rosemary into a cheesecloth or light fabric bag. Place the bag in a Pyrex bowl and add 2½ cups boiling water. Let stand until cool. Bottle and label. To bring out highlights in light hair, follow the same steps with a handful of fresh chamomile.

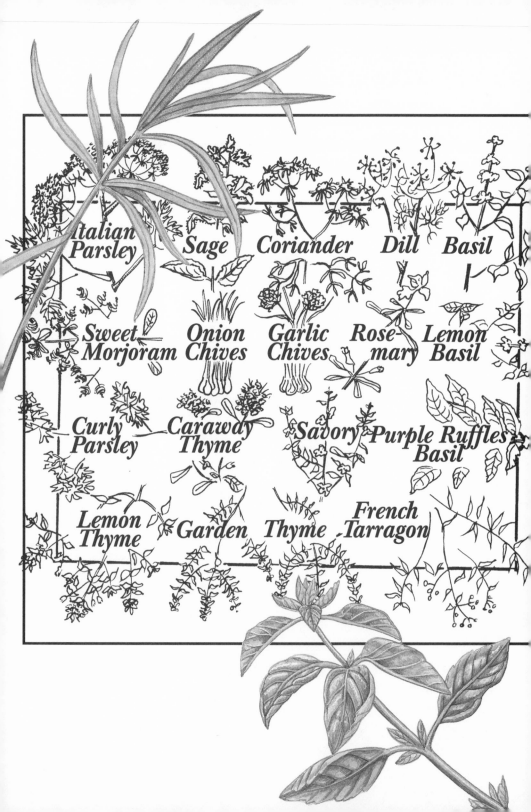

Italian Parsley

Sage

Coriander

Dill

Basil

Sweet Morjoram

Onion Chives

Garlic Chives

Rosemary

Lemon Basil

Curly Parsley

Caraway Thyme

Savory

Purple Ruffles Basil

Lemon Thyme

Garden Thyme

French Tarragon

Growing Herbs in the Kitchen... and Beyond

Herbs are meant to be enjoyed all the year through. In this chapter we'll explain several ways you can bring herbs into your home, kitchen, and yard. We'll talk a little about herb landscaping, and even offer a few suggestions that will make it possible for you to enjoy your favorite herbs in the winter!

Let your imagination go when you are selecting your "house herbs." One of our prettiest kitchen herbs is an annual chamomile that had been accidentally seeded under the greenhouse bench. Whatever herbs you choose, they will be a wonderful addition to your home.

Wintering Herbs

Consider growing herbs in your home through the winter. They will provide beauty, pleasant aromas, and taste as good as they look and smell. Many also have medicinal uses.

You will have to experiment with the environment in your home to find the conditions closest to the sunny summer field that most herbs like. You are in luck if you have a bay window, a skylight or a heated sun porch. We suggest you use your best south or west window and back them up with grow lights.

You can use any fluorescent fixture with a cool white light (identified on the tube). We recommend a 16-hour day with the lights 4 to 5 inches from the plants. It works well to use the sunny south window all day and the grow lights each evening. We find that 72°F during the day and 55°F at night are best.

Use a well-drained potting medium, because no herb likes to have wet feet. Be sure that your pot has a bottom drain hole, and put a few pebbles or pot shards in the bottom to keep the hole from plugging up.

Generally, do not water your herbs until they are dry. The soil surface color will probably get lighter, but do not wait until the plant wilts. Water well, making sure that the water runs through the pot and comes out the drain hole. To check your watering when you are through, lay the pot on its side and gently ease the root ball out without disturbing the top. If you watered right, the whole root (not just the top one-third) will be evenly wet. We like the looks of clay pots for our indoor herbs, but we find that they require more frequent watering because of evaporation through the porous clay.

Don't overfertilize. As a general rule, fertilize once a month during the winter, and more often in the growing season. If the leaves begin to yellow, this means that your plant is hungry. Use either a complete fish emulsion fertilizer or a plant fertilizer at one-half strength. Always be sure to water the plant thoroughly before you fertilize.

Since most houses are quite dry in the winter, mist your herbs with clean water using a small hand sprayer. You can also add humidity to your plants by filling a big cookie sheet with even-sized small rocks, setting your plants on the rocks, and adding water to the cookie sheet. (Just make sure that your pots are held up out of the water!)

A Handy Outdoor Herb Garden In a Box

You can easily build and plant a kitchen herb garden in a 1- by 5-foot cedar box. We'll tell you how, and we'll help you fill that box with 20 to 25 wonderful herbs for your enjoyment throughout the summer.

Imagine the rich full scent of basil on an August afternoon or the taste of fresh-cut chives in your scrambled eggs on Sunday morning. The beauty of this tiny kitchen herb garden is that it is all right there, handy on your deck or beside your back door, where you can breathe in all the wonderful fragrances, enjoy the visual beauty, and, best of all, cook and eat all the delicious flavors. For your herb box, you will need the following materials:

17 feet of 1 inch, cedar board, 12 inches wide, cut into 3 pieces, each 5 feet long, and 2 pieces, each 1 foot long.

1 handful of 6-penny box nails

1 handful of #10 round head screws

NOTE: For those unfamiliar with carpentry, your board will actually be ¾ inch thick and 11¾ inches wide, and you will most likely have to buy 18 feet since lumber yards don't usually sell an odd number of feet. Get rustproof nails and screws–galvanized, chromed, brass, bronze, etc.

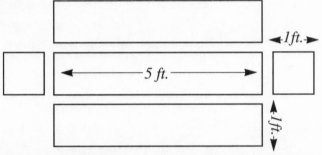

Nail the pieces together, three nails on each side. When secure, put a screw every 12 inches, and 2 in each corner. Drill pilot holes first to prevent splitting the wood.

Drill ⅜ inch holes every 6 inches in the bottom and sides for drainage, putting the side holes about 1 inch above the bottom.

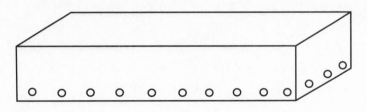

Put the box in full sun. It's a good idea to put in a 1 inch layer of small gravel first, to prevent the holes from being plugged with soil. Then fill the box to within 1 inch of the top with your growing medium. We suggest using one-half garden soil and one-half peat moss, mixed thoroughly. Get in up to your elbows and really stir up a storm! Pulverize those nasty lumps between your hands!

Wet the medium thoroughly, pouring water on it two or three times, waiting a few hours between the waterings to let the water soak down. You want the whole box of medium to be soaked, not just the top few inches. Check the drainage to make sure that you have plenty of holes and they are not stopped up, as you want the water, and air, to percolate down through the soil. If the water cannot drain through the box it will stagnate and drown your plants. Set the box in a place where the drainage won't hurt anything, or arrange for it to be conducted harmlessly away.

There are several ways to fertilize your box. The first method is adding lime. If the soil is a ph of 5 to 6, work in ½ pound of agricultural limestone. If the ph is above 6, do not add limestone since your water may provide enough lime. You can get a ph test from your county agricultural extension service.

Method two is organic fertilizer. Work in dry manure or compost, one peck per box, well before planting time. Then topdress (sprinkle on the soil around the plants) with one peck dry manure or compost three times during the season.

A third method is chemical fertilizer. Work in two ounces of complete fertilizer (20-20-20 or 17-17-17) at planting, and then topdress twice more during the season, but don't get any on the plants.

Another method is water soluble fertilizer. Use it to water the plants once a week, following the manufacturer's recommendations.

Once the danger of frost is past, get some plants from a nursery. Many herbs can be grown from seed, but for this project we recommend that you buy vigorous young plants, preferably in 4 inch pots so they will have a well-developed root system. Thus, your back door herb garden will be beautiful immediately after planting.

You can plant any combination of herbs, but the following is a suggested list:

Basils: 1 sweet basil, 1 minimum basil, 1 lemon basil, 1 cinnamon basil, 1 purple ruffles basil

Thymes: 1 lemon thyme, 1 caraway thyme, 1 garden thyme

Chives: 1 onion chives, 1 garlic chives

Parsleys: 2 Italian parsley, 2 Curly parsley

Miscellania: 1 garden sage, 1 French tarragon, 1 or 2 coriander, 1 summer savory, 1 rosemary (buy as big plant as you can as it grows so slowly) 1 Greek oregano, 1 sweet marjoram, dill

The diagram illustrates how we planted our kitchen herb garden. Many of the basils are tall so we grouped them together. All the thymes, the summer savory, the marjoram, and the oregano trail nicely, so we made sure they were close to the sunshine edge.

Water your little plants thoroughly. If the weather is hot, wait until 5:00 p.m. to transplant. If it is cool and cloudy, any time of the day is okay. Squeeze the 4 inch pot and ease the plant out. Gentleness is important–these are delicate living babies.

With your left hand, scoop a deep hole. The depth of the hole will depend on the size of the root ball, most likely around 4 to 5 inches.

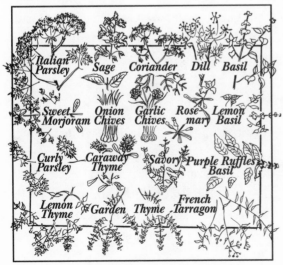

Carefully place the baby plant in the hole, and gently squeeze the soil up around it. Try to disturb the root ball as little as possible.

Continue planting the entire box according to the diagram. You may choose to grow your dill and coriander from seed, being sure to leave spaces for them. Coriander seed

29

is big and easy to handle. Since not all of the seeds you plant are likely to germinate, and it grows well in a clump, we suggest you put 5 to 6 seeds in each spot. Cover with about ¼ inch soil and press lightly. Dill is a little more difficult to germinate. It needs light, so we lay the seeds on the soil surface and cover the area with a small piece of newspaper. Wet down the newspaper and keep it wet until the dill germinates. A few pebbles will keep the newspaper from blowing away.

Next, water your herb garden well. You are on your way! Try not to over-water, but also be sure to not let the plants dry out. Remember that herb gardening is an art, not a science. Believe us, little herb plants are quite forgiving—if you give them half a chance, they will grow.

Soon your herb garden will be big, beautiful, and smell wonderful. The butterflies will flit about it. But don't forget that the main pleasure in a kitchen herb garden is in the eating. So go out with your scissors and snip a little dill, a leaf of basil, and a handful of cilantro for your eating or cooking delight!

An Indoor Herb Window Box

It's also handy to have herbs right under your nose (or your finger-tips) during the summer and winter in a sunny window box above your sink. Follow the basic directions for building the kitchen herb box, adjusting dimensions to fit your particular window. Get a suitable plastic tray to set the box in, to prevent drainage from staining the sill. Fill your box with soil, then fertilize, water, and plant as described above.

Landscaping With Herbs

An herbal meditation pond makes a perfect place to while away a sunny afternoon listening to the bees buzz, watching old Ms. Robin pull up earthworms, and thinking deep thoughts.

For our pond we simply dug a 5- by 10-foot hole six inches deep and lined it with plastic. If you have clay soil or other relatively non permeable soil, you may not need plastic. Of course, you could also install a concrete lining with a drain, but you might want to experiment first before you do something permanent.

We set two big stones at one end, and a large flat rock in the middle. Our first transplanting was a perennial chamomile all the way around the pond. We then set several valerian plants around the big rocks where it now blows gracefully. We put tall wormwood behind the pond next to some sorrel. We planted a large bed of catmint on one side, added a cushion of pennyroyal to perfume our bare feet, and completed our scene with a lovely spread of sweet woodruff on the shady end. As soon as we finished the transplanting, we filled the pond from the hose and sat on up-ended logs to enjoy.

It truly is a magical spot–conducive to slow, even breathing and relaxation. Throughout one particularly dry summer, there was a steady flight of honeybees gathering water to take back to their hives. The daisy-like chamomile blossoms drooped gracefully into the water. As fall came on, the tansy stood proud, showing off its gold buttons, and the catmint pushed out its small purple flowers for its second bloom.

It's a general rule in planting herbs that you can never have too much basil. Try planting a row of perfect little spicy globe basils along the walk to your garage–its perfect spheres will look as if you had pruned them. Try a double row of large sweet basil down the middle of your garden–it will brush against your pant legs as you walk through the garden, releasing its wonderful aroma. Either dark opal basil or purple ruffles will make a lovely purple accent.

Tansy is one of our favorite landscape herbs. It has a full-smelling foliage accented in the fall by the sporty gold buttons. We intersperse tansy on the west side of our house with annual chamomile. Thus, in early summer we have daisy-like blooms peeking through, and the chamomile will self-seed for the following year.

Pennyroyal is a good ground cover in the sun, and it will also survive in partial shade. It has a truly wonderful smell and it helps repel insects. Sweet woodruff is the standby for ground cover in the shade. It has a lovely lacy leaf crown and will spread nicely throughout your shady area where other herbs may not grow.

You might enjoy a clump of tall lovage coming back year after year or a bed of bluish-green rue, the Herb o' Grace. The trailing herbs, such as thyme, nasturtiums, and catmint all add a nice touch to the edges of walks. A rock bed lends itself to chives, parsley, and the thymes.

Herb books are chock full of landscaping ideas that range from complicated knot gardens to simple strawberry pots full of Rosemarinus prostratus and nasturtiums. Try what fits best for you.

Landscaping with herbs is lots of fun. It is a project that provides good smells while you do it, and offers a visual treat throughout summer and fall. Plus, it's edible. Go for it!

BASIL
Ocimum basilicum

CHAPTER 4

Basil

Relax a moment. Close your eyes and imagine that you are resting on a hillside overlooking the sun-dappled Mediterranean Sea. The temperature is a honey-warm 80°F. Butterflies float lazily by, and the light breeze is filled with the rich aroma of basil. You look around, and the entire hillside is carpeted with lush, beautiful basil plants.

You can create this fantasy in your own kitchen. Bring the trapped sunshine of basil into your pastas and salads. Add it to sliced tomatoes and eggplant. Put a little more gusto into your life with basil!

Basils are our best seller and for good reason. They smell good, taste good, and are easy to grow. We grow basils as annuals and plant them from seed. They all perform much the same, although purple ruffles basil is slower than the rest.

There are basil traditions the world over. In parts of Italy, if a young man comes calling with a basil sprig in his lapel, his intentions are serious. On the gory side, Salomé hid John the Baptist's head in a pot of basil. In parts of India, basil is planted around the home to ensure a happy life. According to some people, basil helps keep flying insects out of the house. You may want to experiment with grinding basil leaves and preparing a spray for that purpose. However, in our experience, single plants do not seem to repel flies.

We are not sure where the name basil came from, but it is interesting that in the fourth century AD, the Bishop of Caesarea in Asia Minor, a man active in forming Christian monasteries, was named Basil the Great. Supposedly, the traditions of Indian asceticism and the Buddhist monasteries influenced his work. We understand that holy basil, *Ocimum sanctum*, is planted around temples in India. Several basils come from India and Thailand, perhaps the name originated there.

Cinnamon basil is a nicely shaped plant that grows to be about 18 inches tall and 18 inches wide. It has glossy green leaves and spikes of attractive purple flowers that retain their color all season. The leaves and flowers have a sweet cinnamon flavor and both are edible. The flower stem, however, is quite tough. You can use cinnamon basil as a garnish or as a flavoring in salads, puddings, fruit compotes, and meat dishes. It makes a good potted plant if you have a warm, sunny spot. The dried flower stalk is often used in wreaths, potpourri, and flower arrangements because it retains both color and fragrance when dried. To harvest flowers for drying or for flower arrangements, wait until the flower spike is open halfway up the spike. You can harvest the spikes three or four times a season in Northern climates and more often in warmer states.

Dark opal basil is really a winner of a plant, whether it's in land-scaping, as a potted plant, as a house plant, or as a culinary herb. We think its flavor is sweeter and fuller than most sweet basils. We use the younger leaves in salads, and make a purple pesto sauce for pastas. It makes a beautiful purple vinegar with a bouquet that will knock your socks off. People who have potted dark opal basil for a house plant give it rave reviews as an easy-to-care-for and sweet smelling addition to a sunny window.

Green ruffles basil came on the market as a partner to purple ruffles, but it is not the same type of plant. It has a thicker stem, and the ruffled leaves are closer together. It is much like park seeds' Italian basil or lettuce leaf basil, except for the fact that the leaves are more uniformly shaped. Green ruffles basil can be used much like sweet basil. In landscaping, it would serve as a green foil to purple ruffles.

Lemon basil has a definite lemon scent and flavor. Hairy stems and a lighter green color set it off from the other green basils. The leaves are narrow and the flowers white. It grows about 18 inches high and 12 inches wide. It makes a nice lemon flavored tea and adds lemon flavoring to many recipes. We don't think it is as pretty as the other basils, but the strong lemony scent makes it an aromatic house plant. When brought indoors it, too, needs a sunny spot.

Licorice basil is much more rank and open than the other basils. Fast growing, it may quickly reach 30 inches tall. Its flower spike is a pretty purple and both flowers and leaves have a distinctive licorice flavor and fragrance. Because of its tall stature and pretty spikes, it makes a lovely background plant. The flavor does not hold up in cooking, but licorice basil does well as a garnish or as a fresh addition to fruit salads.

Minimum basil, so called because of its small leaves, grows to be 24 inches tall. Constant pruning of its delicious leaves induces it to grow just as wide. This plant of excellent aroma and flavor is reputedly the choice basil of French cuisine. The flavor falls somewhere between that of anise and cloves. The glossy little leaves make an excellent garnish. Minimum basil is a good doorstep basil because of its faster growth and because it has so many uses. It is also hardier than the other sweet basils, so it can be enjoyed a couple of weeks longer in the fall. This is the basil for pesto lovers.

Purple ruffles basil is a relatively new plant that came on the market in 1986. What we said about dark opal basil is true of purple ruffles also, but we think that purple ruffles is an even more beautiful plant. Its flavor is just as sweet, but it's taste is more anise-like than clove-like. It is a little slower growing, and we think it likes temperatures a bit warmer than the other basils. Its leaves, as the name implies, are ruffly, and, when young, they go well raw in just about any dish wanting a dash of color and a sweet anise flavor. Purple ruffles basil will grow to be abut 24 inches tall, and a little taller than dark opal. It has been used in many seed house trial gardens as a background and accent plant for petunias and other plantings. If we were to choose, purple ruffles would be our first culinary choice of all the basils.

Spicy globe basil is an offspring of minimum basil. It is a beautiful round plant, a sphere of tiny green leaves interspersed with small white flowers. Its leaves and stature are the smallest of the basils. Since it grows to be no taller than 12 inches, it is an excellent border plant. It is both a decorative and a culinary house plant. It is lovely to run your hand over it and smell that divine basil aroma wafting through your kitchen. If you pot up a mature globe basil from your herb garden, you may find the falling blossoms and leaves a little messy. Set the pot in a pie tin to contain them. Snip back the blossoms to keep your plant going. You may wish to bring in a younger plant to get more enjoyment out of it. The spicy globe basil in our kitchen needs water almost every morning, but we find it's worth the extra effort.

Sweet basil must have origins in Italy because many customers at the St. Paul Farmers Market describe it as *Bellissimo*. It is a large-leafed 24 inch plant with flower spikes and glossy green leaves. It is by far our best selling herb, both as a plant and as a cut herb. It is an excellent foil to tomatoes, and can be added to any tomato dish, salad, or stuffed-vegetable dish. We understand that its oils are added to some liqueurs. It is reputedly an insect repellent, and it also has medicinal properties ascribed to it. Many of our friends use the leaves, blended with garlic and pine nuts, to make a Green pesto sauce that makes their pasta come alive. We also recommend trying dark opal or purple ruffles basil for a purple pesto sauce.

Growing

Basil is one of the easiest herbs to grow, and is probably one of the most used culinary herbs. If you are new to growing basil, try the sturdy sweet basil as your mainstay. But don't miss out on the wonderful flavor of purple ruffles for salads. Also, the exotic, perfumed flavor of tulsi sacred is great for stir-frying.

Each year we plant a beautiful basil display garden that includes purple ruffles, green ruffles, sweet, cinnamon, dark opal, and tulsi sacred. We encircled them all with the perky spicy globe basil. On sunny days in August our basil garden is truly a sensual experience, both visually and aromatically. If companion planting interests you, basil has a natural affinity to tomatoes—in the garden and on the plate.

(Companion planting is placing plants close so they can help each other by providing shade and a windbreak. They also help in repelling pests or attracting beneficial insects.)

In mild climates basil is a semi-woody perennial shrub. However, most botanists classify it as an annual. Basil likes a warm sunny position with a well-drained fertile soil and a constant water supply. It cannot stand temperatures below 40°F, and it does not do well in cold winds.

A basil plant needs about 1 square foot of growing space. However, the varieties vary greatly in size, from the tiny-leaved spicy globe, which is barely 10 inches tall, to the large-leaved Genovese sweet basil, which grows 24 inches tall.

Pests don't really bother basils in a small herb garden, but if you grow them in large quantities to sell, there may be some pests that will give you a little competition. We have had a little trouble with grasshoppers grazing in our basil field. In the greenhouse we have had mealy bugs, cutworms, and mildew. We handle the mealy bugs by washing the plants with soapy water, not detergent. We use Ivory hand soap or Fels-Naphtha. Ladybug larvae will also eat the little varmints. You can buy the larvae, but we have discovered that the ladybugs go wherever the food is, so if there aren't enough mealy bugs to fill the ladybugs' tiny tummies, the larvae move on. If there are enough mealy bugs, the lady bugs will move in anyway. Cutworms can be picked off the plants. By keeping trash and vegetation off the greenhouse floor, they will be starved out. If the greenhouse floor is kept clean between crops, the cutworms will not have a chance to start.

Propagating

All of the basils discussed readily root from stem cuttings. To produce basil on a large scale, seeding is preferred. To start basil from seed, we prepare our plastic cell trays, place 3 to 5 seeds on the soil in each cell, and cover them lightly with no more than ¼ inch of vermiculite. Then we wet the tray again and cover it with a sheet of clear plastic. We put the covered trays in a germination unit, warm the soil to

80°F, and maintain the temperature until germination–3 days with most good basil seed.

If you are improvising with no real germination unit, just remember that you are attempting to duplicate the conditions where basil grows best–full sun at 70 to 80°F. The soil temperature is not so critical, as basil will germinate at temperatures ranging from 65 to 95°F. The colder the soil, the longer it takes to germinate. Cool soil produces the short, sturdy plants you want. While seeds germinate faster in warm soil, you will get succulent, leggy plants that you don't want.

Soon after our basils germinate, we remove the trays to the greenhouse where the seedlings grow for about 21 days, whereupon we transplant the entire root-ball contents of each cell to 4-inch pots where the plants grow for another 21 to 25 days. Then they are ready to sell.

If the plants look puny, we give them a shot of fish emulsion at one-half the recommended rate. We keep garbage cans of water in the greenhouse that we add the fish emulsion to and then water the plants with a sump pump.

The basil plants that we intend to transplant to our garden for cut herbs we leave in the cell tray for another 28 days. The next 4 to 5 days we "harden them off" by cutting back on their water and fertilizer, and exposing them to the outdoors, first in a shady area, then in partial sun, and finally in full sun.

When the plants are hardened, we pull them out of the cells and plant the entire root-ball with one foot spacing between them in rows that are 3½ feet apart. (Remember that we planted 3 to 5 seeds in each cell so we plant whatever comes with the root ball, all in one clump.)

If you buy your baby basil plants instead of growing them from seed, the following criteria will help in your selection. The plant should be 6 to 8 inches tall. A 4-inch pot is preferable. The color should be a lusty, dark green or purple, not pale. The roots should be white, and should just reach the edge of the pot. If they go around and around the outside of the root ball and are discolored, the seedling is too old and is going to take longer to get started in your garden. If such plants are all that are available, take your knife and cut a small cut in the rootball in about 4 places equidistant around the root. This cut will trigger the plant to send out secondary roots and it will stop the roots from growing in circles around the root ball. Seedlings that are already flowering are also too old to be of much use in your garden. But, again, if that is all that is available, remove the flower stems and try to get it growing vegetatively again. The stems and leaves should be healthy looking, with no woody stems or discolored leaves. When you transplant your plants, you will get maximum production if you set them out on squares that are 12- by 12-inches or 18- by 18-inches.

If you prefer to directly seed your basil into the garden, wait until you're past the last frost date for your locality, and the average daily temperature reaches 65°F. Prepare your soil and fertilize the same as if you were transplanting seedlings.

You can plant basil in a drill, or you can plant 3 to 5 seeds in a clump at the desired spacing. Allow at least 1 square foot per plant or clump. After the baby basils are up and are 5 or 10 days old, block (thin) your drill to the desired spacing, or thin your clump to the number of plants you want. Pull weeds at the same time.

We sometimes use vermiculite to cover direct seeded basil, but since the seed is small, we cover it to a depth of only ⅛ inch. Then we make sure it does not dry out before germination. Germination is usually in 7 to 12 days here in central Minnesota, in the vicinity of Lake Wobegon. Give your basil crop a steady supply of moisture, as it does not take kindly to moisture stress and will become tough, bitter, and stunted. Mildew can be combated by improving ventilation in the greenhouse so it isn't as damp as a swamp.

Harvesting

To harvest basil through most of the summer, pinch out the leaves at the end of each branch in mid-July. If you look carefully at each branch, you will see where new growth is forming on the left and right sides. Pinch just beyond, leaving that growing area. In 3 or 4 weeks new growth is ready. We harvest sweet basil until mid-September, when we take the whole plant. Through continuous harvesting, the plant gets larger and we have a steady supply of new leaves.

Preserving

To keep basil for a few days in your kitchen, gently rinse the branches with cool water. Shake lightly and place the stems in a glass of water on your counter (not in direct sunlight). They may wilt slightly, but they perk up in a few hours. A gentle touch is important in handling basil, as it turns black from bruising, from lying in water, or from being exposed to cold.

We are partial to the leaves of purple ruffles basil in our wintertime tea. So we dry bunches at the peak of the August harvest. We cut the stems about 9 inches long, rinse them, and hang them upside down to dry, inside, and out of direct sunlight.

Another drying method: Remove individual leaves and place them in a brown paper sack. Gently shake the sack each day. You can also dry basil leaves on paper towels in the refrigerator, or on low settings in an oven or microwave.

Basil butter is good for preserving basil flavor for winter use. The method is the same as for tarragon butter (described on page 74).

Freezing herbs in oil is also popular and works well with basil. Start with 2 cups of clean basil leaves. Be sure they are dry so mold will not form. Chop the basil fine in a food processor or blender, or with a knife. Gradually add ½ cup of olive, peanut, or corn oil. Freeze the mixture in a small container. Scrape off a small amount as you need it, or thaw the entire amount if you are making pesto. Basil vinegar also preserves basil nicely. Green and purple basils work well. Follow the procedure on page 22.

Cooking

Basil has a clove-like, semi-minty aroma to go with its rich, satisfying earthy taste. Use it fresh, of course, and when cooking with it, cook it not at all or for a short time. Once you taste the wonderful flavors of basil with garlic and olive oil, you will soon be an accomplished herbal cook making full-bodied, mouth-watering dishes.

Tomatoes and basil are widely used in Mediterranean cuisine. Sweet basil is great with tomatoes and is also a natural with eggs and cheese. Cinnamon basil and licorice basil are stunning with melon balls and other fruits. One of our favorites is to snip purple ruffles basil and French tarragon over melon balls. We then garnish with the lovely purple blossoms of cinnamon basil. The deep purple of purple ruffles, dark opal, and red holy basil makes perfect garnishes on salads, puddings, and plates of cold cuts. Purple ruffles basil is delicious in salads, adding an anise-like flavor. It is best to start with small amounts.

Italy's Genoa area has a reputation for fine pestos, the green sauces made from basil. If you don't know about pesto, you will learn. A simple meal of a fresh salad, warm bread, red wine, and a hot pasta tossed with basil pesto is a great pleasure. Pesto (pistou) comes from the word pestle, the pounding tool used in a mortar. Traditionally, you make pesto with a mortar and pestle by pounding sliced garlic, pine nuts, salt, and peppercorns. Add basil, parsley, and olive oil, with pounding after each addition. It takes a little time and patience to get a smooth substance. The final step is to fold in Parmesan cheese. For actual measurements see page 44.

Basil herbal tea combines good taste with carminative action. We mix 1 part purple ruffles leaves with 2 parts peppermint and 1 part lemon grass for a delicious purple tea. The tea is wonderful iced in the summer. Add cinnamon basil blossom and a few leaves as a garnish.

If you enjoy dips with fresh vegetables, try this: Blend basil, garlic, and parsley with lemon juice and a touch of salt. Add enough chopped basil and parsley to get the taste you want, then fold the mixture into about a cup of mayonnaise.

❦ Sliced Tomatoes with Basil ❦

This classic combination of basil leaves with freshly sliced tomatoes weds two robust summertime treats into a very special dish.

1 large, vine-ripened tomato (room temperature)
1 sweet onion
2 tablespoons freshly cut basil leaves, roughly chopped
1 tablespoon wine vinegar
salt and coarse ground black pepper

Cut tomato and onion into ¼-inch thick slices. Arrange in an overlapping pattern on your prettiest plate. Sprinkle with wine vinegar and basil leaves. Season and let stand 30 minutes at room temperature before serving.

Sometimes we add a sprinkle of feta cheese crumbs and a garnish of purple ruffles basil leaves.

❦ Melon Patch Pesto ❦

Probably the most popular way to preserve basil is to make pesto and freeze it. The usual procedure is to omit the Parmesan cheese until the pesto is thawed. Then fold in the Parmesan just before tossing the pesto with the pasta.

In a blender, combine ⅓ cup olive oil, 3 cloves peeled-and-chopped garlic, 2 tablespoons pine nuts, and ½ teaspoon salt. Blend until smooth. Add 2 cups fresh basil leaves and ½ cup fresh parsley. Blend well. Place mixture in bowl, and gently fold in ½ cup grated Parmesan. Toss with hot spaghetti and serve at once.

If you make pesto with a mortar and pestle, do not add the oil too soon. Make a paste of garlic, pine nuts, and salt before alternately adding small amounts of olive oil, basil, and parsley. We like enjoying a glass of good red wine with our guests while hand-pounding the pesto. It stimulates the taste buds!

Once you have mastered basic pesto, try variations. Some people prefer less expensive walnuts to pine nuts. Make a purple pesto using purple ruffles basil. Three tablespoons of fresh oregano leaves can add variety, as can minced sun-dried tomatoes or a cup of mint leaves. A cilantro pesto is good on chops or steaks. Occasionally we add a bit of sorrel for a lemony, sharp taste.

❦ Easy Stuffed Tomatoes ❦

Stuff tomato halves with 2 to 3 green onions, a boiled egg, 1 tablespoon each fresh basil, and fresh parsley, all chopped. Add a bit of butter, ½ cup oatmeal, and the chopped pulp of the tomatoes. Top each half with grated Parmesan, and bake at 350° for 30 to 35 minutes. Garnish with fresh basil.

❦ Stuffed Tomatoes 2 ❦

4 to 6 Servings

6 large ripe, firm tomatoes
8 ounce mild Italian sausage, casing removed
¾ cup chopped onion
2 cloves garlic, minced
⅔ cup diced zucchini
2 tablespoons chopped fresh basil
1 tablespoon each red wine vinegar and chopped fresh oregano
½ teaspoon salt
¼ teaspoon pepper
1½ cups cooked rice
½ cup (2 ounce) shredded Provolone cheese
6 tablespoons freshly grated Parmesan cheese, divided
3 tablespoons chopped fresh parsley

Preheat oven to 350°. Slice tops off tomatoes and discard. Using a small knife, remove pulp from tomatoes, leaving the shell intact. Discard seeds. Chop pulp and reserve. Invert tomato shells onto paper toweling to drain. Cook sausage, onion, and garlic until sausage is brown and crumbly. Drain off excess fat. Stir in reserved tomato pulp, zucchini, basil, vinegar, oregano, salt, and pepper. Simmer, uncovered, for 10 minutes. Remove from heat. Stir in rice, Provolone, 4 tablespoons Parmesan cheese, and parsley. Place tomato shells in a 2-quart rectangular baking dish. Spoon filling into shells, mounding the top. Sprinkle with remaining 2 tablespoons of Parmesan cheese. Bake 25 to 30 minutes, or until hot and bubbly. Serve immediately. *(Courtesy of the United Dairy Association.)*

❧ Easy Tomato Salad with Basil ❧

Cut 4 ripe tomatoes into wedges. Arrange on a pretty serving plate. Pour 2 tablespoons olive oil over them. Add 1 minced clove garlic, 1 teaspoon snipped chives, and several sliced scallions. Top with equal parts of rough-chopped sweet basil and purple ruffles basil (about 2 tablespoons each). Refrigerate ½ hour, toss, and serve.

❧ New Potatoes with Basil Butter ❧

1 pound small red potatoes
1 tablespoon butter
¼ teaspoon fresh garlic, minced
dash of cayenne pepper
1 tablespoon heavy cream
1 tablespoon chopped fresh basil
salt and pepper to taste

Steam potatoes 12 to 15 minutes, until tender. Melt butter over low heat and stir in the garlic, cream, and cayenne. Remove from heat and add basil. Cut potatoes in half, place in a warm serving dish, and gently pour the basil butter over the potatoes. Season with salt and pepper.

❧ Eggplant with Basil ❧

1 eggplant, peeled and cut into cubes
1 large onion, chopped
6 tablespoons olive oil
3 tablespoons fresh basil leaves, chopped
salt and fresh ground pepper to taste.

Saute ingredients in olive oil for 5 to 6 minutes. Cover and cook until the eggplant is tender, stirring frequently. Add water if necessary. (You may have noticed that we find the taste of peppercorns, freshly ground in a pepper mill, to be far superior to the powdered product.)

❧ Cream of Tomato Soup with Basil Garnish ❧

2 cups fresh tomatoes, skinned and chopped
½ cup chopped celery
1 small white onion, chopped
1 teaspoon honey
2 tablespoons butter
2 tablespoons flour
1 cup milk

Combine tomatoes, celery, onion, and honey in a saucepan. Simmer 15 minutes, covered. While mixture simmers, combine butter and flour in small saucepan over low heat. Add milk, increase heat to medium, and stir constantly until white sauce begins to thicken. Remove from heat. Add the tomato mixture, salt, and coarse ground black pepper. Top each bowl with 1 teaspoon fresh basil, snipped fine with scissors.

❧ *Lemon Basil Herbs and Spice Substitute* ❧

1 teaspoon celery seed
¼ teaspoon grated dried lemon peel
½ teaspoon paprika
2 tablespoons dried lemon basil or dill weed, finely crumbled
2 tablespoons toasted sesame seeds
a pinch of freshly ground pepper
½ teaspoon garlic powder
1 teaspoon dried oregano leaves, crumbled
2 tablespoons onion powder

Combine ingredients thoroughly. Place in a small air-tight container. Great for soups, sauces, and vegetables. *(Contributed by the Minnesota Grown Program.)*

CHIVES
Allium schoenoprasum

CHAPTER 5

Chives

Onion chives are one of the first herbs up in the spring. Look for the dark green tubular stems that have a mild, sweet, onion-like taste and aroma. The leaves are hollow and the flowers are globe-shaped and purple. Garlic chives are slower to arrive. Late spring frosts keep nipping their leaves, but they keep coming. By late May or early June, earlier in other parts of the country, they are ready as a flavoring and garnish. We grow two species of chive plants: onion (or garden) chives and garlic chives (also called Chinese leeks). Both are hardy perennials, at least as far north as Zone 3. Once established, chives last many years. We still have chives that were planted 13 years ago around our house foundation. Chives are a foolproof herb; ours are about as ignored and abused as a plant can be!

Growing

Plant in a weed-free area. Chives compete well with weeds, but weeds make it difficult to use chives, particularly if grass grows between the chive leaves. Chives like a well drained, sunny spot in your herb garden, but they tolerate lesser conditions. Chives are excellent in borders. After you see them in full blossom, you will want them in your landscaping scheme.

For some reason garlic chives are not hardy in the North their first year so if you buy seeds or seedlings, you must mulch them the first year after the ground freezes. Remove the mulch in late April. From then on, no mulch will be required. You also won't have to mulch if you buy sets, since they are already winter hardy. Onion chives will never need mulch.

The best way to have chives year-round is to divide a clump in late August and pot them so they can establish themselves. Use a large pot, 6-inch or so. It's okay to trim some of the roots so the plant will fit in the pot. After the winter freeze, place the chives where they will remain frozen, such as the north side of a building or in some heavily mulched spot, then mulch them or put them in a cold frame where it will not get below 0°F, and let them rest for 6 weeks. About 2 weeks before you want chives, bring the pot indoors and place it in a sunny window. You can take several crops of chives from a pot before it starts to decline. At that time, return it to a protected spot outdoors for replanting in spring. Allow it to rejuvenate in the summer, and start the process over again in late August.

A Chinese trick to protect garlic chives from spring frostbite is to cover the plants with a straw mulch about 18 inches thick. The mulch protects the leaves and excludes light. The result is yellow chives, not found in supermarkets but considered a delicacy in China. The process is much like growing white asparagus or a Belgian endive. You can also do this by growing potted chives covered with another pot to exclude light. Depending on the temperature, it will take 7 to 28 days to produce leaves tall enough to use.

Propagating

If you choose to start your chives from sets, get enough sets to make a handful of chive leaves in each clump to harvest. Both onion and garlic chives multiply so you have to divide the clumps every 3 years. Move them to new soil to regenerate them.

If you choose to grow your chives from seed, make sure the seed is fresh; it is not viable for long. Use a 4-inch pot. Sprinkle the seed over the entire top of the soil if you want a large clump for either selling or transplanting into your garden. Use bottom heat of 75 to 80°F, and let the plants grow for 8 weeks before transplanting.

Harvesting

You can start harvesting either type of chives as soon as the leaves are long enough to grasp. Cut the desired amount right to the ground. Harvest the entire clump at once, if you wish. In the peak growing season, more chives will be back for harvest in 2 or 3 weeks.

Garlic chive blossoms are edible as buds, flowers, and flat green seed capsules that form after pollination. The white blossoms are a great cut flower, and they also dry for everlastings.

Harvest onion chive flowers in the bud stage, and use them as a seasoning in soup, salad, and vegetable dishes. When buds first open, they are edible and make a beautiful garnish. Harvest them, and garlic chive blossoms, by cutting the entire plant at ground level and separating flower stems from the leaves. The flower stems are tender enough to eat in the bud stage, but they become tough and straw-like when the flowers open. At this point, gather and dry them for use in everlasting bouquets.

Preserving

Freezing is the best way to preserve the flavor. Chop chives and blend them with cooking oil (⅓ to ½ cup of oil for 2 cups of chives). Freeze in small glass jars. In recipes we use the same amount of this blend as we use of fresh chives.

You can also freeze chives without oil. Freeze chive bunches, each about ½ inch in diameter, in plastic freezer bags. When you want chives, remove them from the bag and cut with scissors into the dish.

Use onion chives in herb vinegars, usually with other herbs. Use the lavender blossoms to color garlic, basil, tarragon, or salad burnet vinegar. Onion and garlic chives, alone or with other herbs, make fine herb butters. Chives do not retain much flavor when dried, so we do not recommend drying.

Cooking

If you believe, like we do, that texture and visual presentation play a part in how something tastes, then chives will play an important part in your culinary artistry. You can crush, cut, curl, or tie the fresh leaves. You can use the lavender blossoms of onion chives that arrive in May (in our part of the country) as a fresh-cut flower. Chives add a sharp, non-offensive onion-like flavor to soups and salads, and will meld with a host of other seasonings. You can also use this member of the *Allium* genus as a dye for herbal vinegars or a garnish with many dishes.

When the white, star-shaped, rose-smelling flowers of garlic chives arrive in August, you will have additional tasty garnishing and seasoning material. The flowers have a different texture, but they taste like the leaves.

When cooking with chives, remember that they lose their flavor when heated. Add them only for the last minute of cooking, or wait until the dish has finished cooking. Chop chives fine and add them to soups, salads, creamed or sauced vegetables, cottage or creamed cheese, sour cream, or sandwich spreads. Chives are delicious atop eggs, chops, or steaks, when mixed into scrambled eggs and potato salad, and as a garnish on anything that is set off well by a bright green color. As a garnish, their flat leaves can be cut into interesting shapes.

Here are several chive recipes that we've grown to like:

❧ Chives and Sour Cream with Baked Potato ❧

8 ounces sour cream
½ cup chopped onion chives
6–8 medium baking potatoes
salt and pepper to taste

Mix chopped chives in sour cream just before serving (or several days ahead if you store in the refrigerator). Serve at room temperature with baked potatoes hot from the oven. Make a long slit in the top of each, squeeze open, and put on a generous dollop of the sour cream-chive mixture. Sprinkle with salt and pepper.

❧Scrambled Eggs with Yellow Garlic Chives❧

4 eggs
½ pound yellow garlic chives
½ teaspoon pepper
4 green onions
½ teaspoon salt
2 tablespoons butter or oil

Heat butter or oil in a skillet over medium-low heat until butter melts. Add chopped onions and saute until onions are limp. Break eggs into the onions and butter. Add chopped chives, salt, and pepper. (We use kitchen scissors to cut chives and green onions into ¼-inch pieces.) Stir until eggs are set. Serve. A halved cherry tomato or a Johnny jump-up make a nice garnish for this dish.

*You can substitute green garlic chives for yellow ones. See the text on yellow garlic chives; you will have to grow your own.

❧Herb Butter❧

See page 21 for general instructions on making herb butter. For Garlic Herb Butter, blend ¼ pound of softened butter with 2 large crushed garlic cloves and one well packed teaspoon of finely cut onion or garlic chives. Use on baked potatoes, chops, steaks, broiled or poached fish fillets, and in egg dishes. The combination enhances the flavor. The butter can be refrigerated for several days or frozen for longer times. Use herbs in place of salt and pepper to enhance the flavor of your dishes.

❧ Stir-Fried Daikon ❧

The daikon radish, a Melon Patch specialty, is a long, white-fleshed Oriental radish. It tastes like the little red one, but it is zippier and crisper.

1 pound daikon radish
2 tablespoons cooking oil
1 teaspoon sugar
dash of salt
1 tablespoon chopped parsley
1 tablespoon chopped garlic chives

Cut daikon into thin half-moon slices. In a wok or large skillet heat oil to medium high. Add sliced daikon, sugar, and salt. Stir-fry until slightly translucent, about 5 minutes. Stir in parsley and chives. Serve.

❧ Beef Stew with Daikon ❧

In this typical Midwestern beef stew, daikon replaces the rutabagas or parsnips.

2 pounds beef rump or chuck
2 tablespoons cooking oil
2 cloves garlic, minced or crushed
1 large onion, sliced
2 teaspoons beef bouillon, or 2 bouillon cubes
2 cups water
1 tablespoon molasses
1 teaspoon fennel seed
3 large potatoes
3 large carrots
1 daikon radish (1½ lb.)
2 tablespoons chopped chives

Cut beef into 1-inch cubes. Heat the oil in Dutch oven. Stir in beef and garlic. Add the onion, water, bouillon, fennel seed, and molasses. Cover and bake at 350° for 1½ hours. Cut the daikon, potatoes, and carrots into 1-inch cubes. Add the cubes to stew. Cover and simmer for about 30 minutes or until vegetables are tender. Mix in the chopped chives and serve.

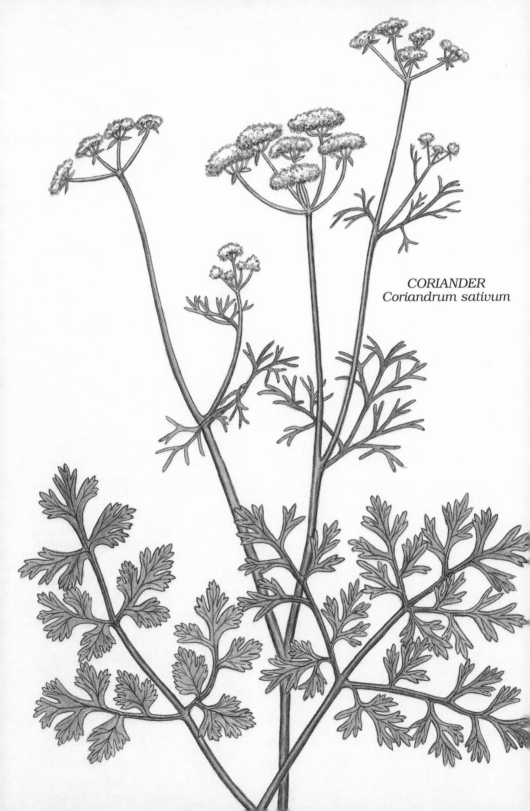

CORIANDER
Coriandrum sativum

Coriander, Cilantro, and Chinese Parsley

Coriander, cilantro, and Chinese parsley are all names for the same citrus-spicy, sage-flavored plant. For thousands of years this bright green plant with the bold fragrance and taste has thrilled some people and left others less enthusiastic.

The plant is used culinarily for its young leaves, ripened seeds, and roots. We call the leaf and root cilantro, which has a distinct flavor from the seed, which is called coriander.

The word coriandrum comes from the Greek word, *koris*, a type of bug. That may explain the fetid smell of the leaves. To the uninitiated, the plant's smell and taste are quite disagreeable, often musky. As the plant matures, its seeds develop a full, tangy flavor. Coriander seeds have been found in Egyptian tombs, the ancient Hebrews are said to have used them in Passover, and the Chinese believe that the seeds confer immortality.

Cilantro is a Spanish name for this ancient herb. By the way, some call cilantro an herb and coriander a spice.

When we first grew coriander, we noticed an unpleasant aroma in our garden. We traced it to the plant. Our thought was: "We'll never grow this stuff again. Nobody would touch anything smelling this bad!" We didn't grow it for 2 years, but our customers kept asking for it. Since "grow what your customers want" is one of the secrets to a farmer's success, we now grow a nice patch every year. We eventually tried some Mexican and Oriental dishes flavored with coriander after a Thai friend told us how good it is. Then we learned that it is an ingredient in the bread-and-butter pickles we had been making for years. We now love it and we recommend coriander highly, even though we still cannot describe the unique flavor.

Growing

Coriander, a small annual, grows 1 to 2 feet tall and has a rounded, finely grooved stem. Its lower leaves are rounded, slightly toothed, bright green, and glabrous. Use these leaves, not the feathery, thinner, more mature leaves. The mauve-white flower is a flat compound umbrel (umbrella-like) that attracts pollinating insects. The seed is round, small, pea shaped, and easy to plant. We plant it in a constant drill, 10 seeds per foot. We do multiple plantings every 2 weeks from late April to early August, and we do not thin our plantings. The August planting is about three times larger than the earlier ones since cold fall temperatures do not bother it. Hot weather tends to cause seeds to stalk and bolt, but the Santo variety is said to bolt less quickly. In the heat of summer, it helps to grow coriander in light shade rather than full sun.

Coriander grows especially well in the cool of spring and fall. With normal fall temperatures, it should grow through October. You can transplant coriander, but a large plant quickly goes to seed.

Propagating

Coriander is grown from seed, usually directly seeded into the garden. We do transplant a lot of it, for easy weed control. About 9 weeks after germination it will start sending up its seed stalk in high summer. This is not the case in late spring or early fall. The plant remains vegetative and doesn't flower. We recommend multiple plantings so that lush cilantro is available all season.

Harvesting

Harvest cilantro when leaves are young, rounded, and green. We sometimes cut the plant just to the growing point, thus getting about three cuttings. Usually we uproot the whole plant when it is about 6 inches tall. Wash off dirt and place the plant in water in the kitchen for brief storage. It will keep in prime condition for over a week. Use the leaves whole or lightly chopped. We generally use them raw or only slightly cooked.

To harvest coriander seeds, leave them on the plant until they begin turning brown. Do not wait too long, however, or they will fall. Cut the entire plant, place it in a brown sack, and hang it upside down. Shake it occasionally until all the seeds release. Store seeds in a dry, cool place, and do not crack them until you are ready to use them. The roots, a flavorful treat, are usually washed and pounded in a mortar with a pestle. You can also finely mince them with garlic and add to marinades. The roots have a citrus flavor with nutty overtones. They are often used in Thai recipes and their flavor blends quite well with lemon grass.

Preserving

Cilantro leaves do not dry well, as they lose their flavor. Fresh cilantro is best, without question, but you can freeze unblanched leaves, either plain or in oil. You can freeze bruised or pounded roots, since they retain more flavor than the leaves.

You can grind ripe seeds into powder for use in baking or curries. Or you can crack seeds and use them to flavor fruits and desserts. They can also be roasted and cracked, or used whole. Some say roasting makes them more flavorful.

Cooking

Coriander/cilantro in any form is good in dressings, marinades, brines, stews, or sauces. You can add it to salads, potatoes, onions, or sausage, so acquiring a taste for it is definitely worth the effort. Coriander is used as a meat preservative and a flavoring in liqueurs and gin. Cilantro is used in Mexican, Southeast Asian, Chinese, Turkish, East Indian, and Spanish cuisines, among others. It also is good in English chutney when mixed with apples, mint, and ginger.

You can make a flavorful curry powder by combining equal parts of powdered coriander, powdered ginger, and powdered cardamon (about 1 ounce each) with 3 ounces of turmeric and dried cayenne pepper to taste. Rice dishes with beans also benefit from coriander or cilantro. An omelette is much enhanced with chopped fresh cilantro and a touch of salsa. Cilantro is good in spinach or lettuce salads, and your guests will be all smiles if you gently toss cilantro leaves with your fruit salad.

Whether you make soup from scratch or open a can to heat for lunch, experiment with adding ½ teaspoon of crushed coriander seeds to either tomato or chunky chicken soup. Also, float a couple of teaspoons of fresh cilantro leaves on top.

Having apple pie and coffee for dessert? A teaspoon of crushed coriander seeds accents the pie nicely. And to make a wonderfully flavored coffee, brew it strong and add freshly crushed coriander seeds and a bit of honey. For an initial taste of cilantro, try the following recipe, which our daughter Jacque and her husband Doug introduced to us.

❧ Jacque and Doug's Whole Wheat ❧ Tortillas with Cilantro

Makes 1 tortilla

¼ cup green cilantro leaves, chopped
¼ cup red onion, chopped
¼ cup refried beans, heated
¼ cup Monterey Jack cheese, grated

Warm a soft, whole wheat tortilla on one side in a frying pan over low heat. Turn it over. Add onion, cheese, beans, and cilantro. Heat on low until cheese begins melting. Add a liberal amount of your favorite hot sauce (salsa cruda, picante). Fold and serve.

❧ Tomato-Cilantro Chicken ❧

Serves 4

4 skinless, boned chicken breast halves (about 1 pound), slightly flattened
1 medium onion, chopped (½ cup)
1¼ pounds ripe tomatoes, sliced (about 4 medium)
4 ounces part-skim mozzarella or farmers cheese, shredded
1 tablespoon lime juice
½ teaspoon salt
⅛ teaspoon ground red pepper
2 teaspoons olive oil
1 clove garlic, finely chopped
½ cup chopped green pepper
¼ cup chopped fresh cilantro
cilantro leaves and lime slices for garnish (optional)

Preheat oven to 400°. Combine lime juice, ¼ teaspoon salt, and red pepper in small bowl. Add chicken. Turn to coat. Let stand 10 minutes. Heat 1 teaspoon oil in a non-stick skillet over medium heat. Add chicken, and saute until lightly browned on both sides. Remove to paper toweling to drain. Add remaining 1 teaspoon oil to skillet. Add onion, green pepper, and garlic. Saute until tender but not browned, stirring often. Remove from heat. Stir in cilantro. Place about ⅔ of tomato slices on bottom of 9-inch square baking dish. Sprinkle with ⅔ of onion mixture and remaining ¼ teaspoon salt. Sprinkle with ⅔ of the cheese. Add chicken breasts. Top with remaining tomato slices and onion mixture. Bake 15 to 20 minutes, or until chicken is tender. Sprinkle with remaining cheese. Bake 5 minutes longer to melt cheese. Garnish with cilantro leaves and lime slices, if you wish. You can also bake the chicken in individual dishes. Lower baking time to 10 to 15 minutes. *(Contributed by the Minnesota Grown Program.)*

❧ West Coast Turkey Chili ❧

Serves 6

1 cup green pepper, chopped
2 cloves garlic, minced
2 cans (15½-ounces each) kidney beans, drained
1 cup red wine
1 tablespoon fresh cilantro, chopped or 1 teaspoon dried
½ teaspoon salt
1¼ cups onion, chopped
3 tablespoons vegetable oil
1 can (28 ounces) stewed tomatoes, crushed
3 cups cooked turkey, cut into ½-inch cubes
1 teaspoon crushed red pepper

In a 3-quart saucepan over medium heat, saute green pepper, onion, and garlic in oil 5 minutes or until vegetables are tender-crisp. Add beans, tomatoes, wine, turkey, chili powder, cilantro, red pepper, and salt. Increase heat to high and bring mixture to boil. Reduce heat to low and simmer mixture, uncovered, 25 minutes. To serve, garnish with fresh cilantro. *(Contributed by National Turkey Federation.)*

❧ Fruit Salad with Cilantro ❧

Serves 6

Stir together and set aside:
4 ounces sour cream
2 tablespoons maple syrup

CHOP FINE:
¼ cup pecans
1 bunch cilantro leaves

CUT UP:

2 apples
2 oranges, peeled
2 bananas, peeled
2 kiwi fruit, peeled
1 bunch seedless green grapes

Combine fruit and pecans in bowl. Add cilantro and ¼ cup coconut. Toss gently. Serve in small individual bowls with a dollop of the sour cream-maple syrup mixture on top. Garnish it with fresh cilantro leaves.

Brown Rice with Cilantro and Almonds

Serves 4

Rice is an important food in our home.
This recipe is a simple, delicious rice dish.

1 cup brown rice
2 cups water
salt, a pinch
½ teaspoon butter
½ teaspoon slivered almonds
½ cup fresh cilantro leaves, finely snipped with scissors

Mix water, brown rice, salt, and butter in a 2-quart saucepan. Bring to a boil. Stir. Cover and reduce heat to low. Cook, covered, for 50 minutes or until rice is tender. Remove from heat and let stand, covered, for 10 minutes. Toss lightly with the chopped cilantro leaves and almonds. Serve.

❧Easy Curry with Coriander Seeds❧ and Fresh Peas

Serves 4

This combines well with the brown rice dish above.
Make it when fresh peas are available.

1 large onion, chopped
3 tablespoons butter
3 medium fresh tomatoes, peeled and quartered
1 small red chili pepper (seeds removed) chopped fine
2 bay leaves (remove after cooking)
2 teaspoons each crushed coriander seeds, ground cumin, and
    turmeric
4 medium potatoes, peeled and quartered
1½ cups water
1 cup freshly shelled peas
salt and coarsely ground black pepper to taste

Fry onion in butter until soft and slightly transparent. Add herbs, spices, tomatoes, potatoes, water, and seasoning. Cook until potatoes are nearly done, about 20 minutes. Add shelled peas the last 5 minutes. For additional spiciness, add more crushed coriander seeds or more red chili pepper.

❧ Stir-Fried Steak with Cilantro ❧

This dish is nice with steamed vegetables.

1 pound sirloin steak, slightly frozen
2 tablespoons oil
2 cloves garlic, minced
3 to 4 roots cilantro, minced
½ cup green onions, chopped, tops and all
1 cup cilantro leaves, chopped

Place steak in freezer until firm, and slice into 1/4-inch strips. (Steak may be sliced several hours ahead and marinated in sauce of your choice.) Stir-fry minced garlic and cilantro roots in oil about 2 minutes. Remove them from oil. Stir-fry ½ the steak at a time for about 3 minutes, removing after cooking. Return meat, garlic-cilantro root mixture, and green onions to frying pan. Stir-fry 30 seconds. Salt and pepper to taste.

❧ Salsa-Topped Burgers ❧

Serves 4

Grilled hamburgers, a summer favorite, with a zesty salsa containing cilantro.

Burgers: Shape 1 pound lean ground beef into four ½-inch thick patties. Grill 10 minutes for medium, or to desired doneness, turning once. Season with salt and pepper after turning.

SALSA:
1 medium tomato, seeded and coarsely chopped
1 tablespoon thinly sliced green onion
1½ teaspoons fresh cilantro, chopped
1½ teaspoons red wine vinegar
1 small garlic clove, minced
⅛ teaspoon each salt and coarsely ground black pepper
½ to 1 jalapeño pepper, seeded and minced
1 cup thinly sliced lettuce

Combine all ingredients except lettuce. Cover and set aside. Place burgers on bottom half of toasted hamburger bun. Top each with equal amounts of salsa and lettuce. Cover with bun tops. *(Contributed by Beef Industry Council.)*

❧ Turkey Fajitas with Spicy Cilantro Sauce ❧

Serves 4

You can do most of this recipe ahead of time. Enjoy time with your guests!

1 pound boneless turkey breast
8 whole wheat tortillas (7-inch)

MARINADE:
¼ teaspoon pepper, coarsely ground
¼ teaspoon salt
1 clove garlic, minced
1 small red chili pepper, seeded and minced
2 tablespoons lime juice
2 tablespoons fresh cilantro leaves, chopped
1½ tablespoons oil

SALSA:
3 ripe tomatoes, chopped
1 tablespoon red onion, chopped
2 tablespoons fresh cilantro leaves, chopped
1 clove garlic, minced
1 jalapeño pepper, seeded and chopped
dash salt

GARNISHES:
3 cups lettuce, torn into small pieces
1 pound cooked black beans
½ cup sour cream
1 avocado, sliced
4 ounces Monterey Jack cheese, shredded

Season turkey with marinade ingredients. Allow to marinate several hours or overnight in a covered container in the refrigerator, opening it once or twice to turn the turkey.

Combine salsa ingredients in a small bowl and let stand at room temperature for 1 hour. Preheat broiler. Broil marinated turkey 10 minutes on each side. Cut into thin strips. Wrap tortillas in foil and warm in oven 6 minutes while turkey cooks.

Place all garnishes and salsa on the table. Serve warmed tortillas and turkey so guests can make their own fajitas.

Play your best mariachi tape or CD and go for the gusto!!

FRENCH TARRAGON
Artemisin drancunculus

French Tarragon

French tarragon, *Artemisia Dracunculus L. var. sativa*, is highly favored by gourmet cooks who use it to flavor many sauces, vinegars, seafood, chicken, egg dishes, steaks, and chops. It is also delicious in marinades and salads. Fresh French tarragon causes a numbing sensation on the tongue. Its aroma is faint, so you must taste the plant to appreciate it. This aroma asserts itself when you heat the herb. Heating increases the aroma but stops the numbing sensation. The wonderful licorice flavor remains, though, combining with foods to produce a unique sweet flavor. When used unheated, as in a fruit salad, French tarragon tends to make the fruit taste sweeter.

Growing

Tarragon is a hardy, vigorous (but not aggressive) perennial. It becomes a bush-like plant, growing in 3 or 4 years to about 2 feet across and 3 feet tall, if unharvested. Its flowers are small, green and white dots that grow in the leaf axils in the top one foot of the plant. Tarragon likes sunny, well drained fertile soil, neutral to slightly alkaline.

The so-called "Tarragon Seed" sold by seed persons is nothing more than a weed, and it has no culinary use. So don't try to grow it from seed, as you will be disappointed unless you really want another weed in your garden. Our advice is to taste French tarragon plants before you buy them. Many supposedly reputable garden centers, chain store garden departments, and landscape nurseries mistakenly substitute Russian tarragon seed for French tarragon, but the Russian variety has no flavor.

Tarragon is hardy, but we do mulch it. After we harvest the entire above-ground part of the plant, we wait until the ground is frozen. Then we put spruce or pine boughs over the tarragon, and cover the boughs with rye straw, making sure the mulch won't blow off. Sometimes, early snow has prevented us from mulching our tarragon, and it has survived, but some of our friends and customers have not been so lucky and they have lost their plants. Remove the mulch gradually over 4 to 5 days, if new growth shows. If not, remove the entire mulch.

Even in northern winters you can grow tarragon in your house or greenhouse, but it does take some management as it requires a rest period. To pot for household use, pot up a plant in late July or early August and let it grow until freeze-up. Then place it in an unheated garage or cold frame for 6 weeks. Don't worry about some brown leaves on the lower stalk, they're natural. Cut off the old dead growth and bring the potted plant, root and crown, into the house and put it where it will get 16 hours of light a day. If it gets less light, it will grow in a rosette and not branch out. The light does not have to be natural; fluorescent white lights emit the correct wavelength to make the plant elongate. You can grow a greenhouse crop of tarragon in pots. Give the plants a 6 week cool treatment of 40°F, and then grow them at 65°F with light 16 hours per day.

Propagating

Tarragon is a sterile clone and can be reproduced only vegeta-tively. That is, it may only be propagated by dividing last year's plant or by taking cuttings from a parent plant. See page 10 for general instructions on these two methods. When a plant reaches 3 to 4 inches tall, we start taking 2- to 3-inch cuttings, taking the leaves off from the bottom to halfway up the cutting. After washing them, we stick the cuttings in a tray of Cornell mix, which has been fortified with extra calcium sulfate, 2 tablespoons per cubic foot, to stimulate rooting. We then place the cuttings under a white plastic cover with a bottom heat of 75°F. Generally, we keep the air temperature between 75 to 85°F. Rooting usually starts in 3 to 4 weeks.

To increase by division, take 3- to 4-year-old plants and divide them as soon as it is warm enough to remove the mulch in the spring. After taking the mulch off, give the soil time to thaw. As soon as the soil has thawed to a depth of about 18 inches, dig up the plants, gently wash the soil off the roots, and divide the roots into as many plants as you can get. Try to divide each crown so that each piece will have some root attached. Pot these divisions into 4 and 6-inch pots, depending on the size of the root clump. The larger the roots and crown, the bigger your plant will be. We grow these divisions in the greenhouse until Mid-May and then replant them in the garden, where we've already prepared a place free of perennial weeds.

Harvesting

Tarragon is one of the first herbs harvested each spring. Begin harvesting when the plant is 2 or 3 inches high. You can take the stems and tips from plants of any age, as long as the plant is growing vigorously. We harvest about ⅔ of the plant nearly to the ground, but we leave at least ⅓ of the plant. Around the beginning of July we harvest the entire plant, cutting it off at ground level. Use this bounty for vinegars and freezing for winter. New growth produces fresh plants to harvest the rest of the season. At the end of September take the whole plant for final harvest. This tarragon is not as flavorful as the July harvest, so use your July harvest for preserving purposes.

Preserving

To preserve tarragon, you can try drying. However, dried tarragon loses the numbing sensation and retains only a mild anise flavor, much like fennel seed. To dry, make small bunches of tarragon and place them in a dark, 70°F environment. Store dried bunches in a dark, dry environment, or freeze them (see section below). Finely crush the leaves when ready to use.

Herb vinegars convert tarragon's flavor and aroma to a longer-lasting product. See page 22 for general instructions on making vinegars. We stuff a wide-mouthed pint or quart glass jar full of tarragon stems and leaves, roughly chopped. Then we fill the jar with cider vinegar and let this mixture set for a week at room temperature. We strain the vinegar and it is ready to use.

To freeze, harvest stems (with their leaves) that are tender enough to snip with your fingernails. Strip the leaves from stems too tough to snip. Lay stems and leaves on cookie sheets (not layered), and freeze. Place frozen herbs in plastic freezer bags, remove as much air as possible, and place the bags in the freezer until you use the herbs. We think the flavor is quite satisfactory.

To keep tarragon for a shorter time—up to a week, for instance—place the cut stems in a glass of water, cover loosely with a plastic bag, and place in the refrigerator. To preserve tarragon's taste in herb butter, add about four tablespoons of cut-and-crushed fresh tarragon to one pound of softened butter. Mix and roll into a cylinder and refrigerate. Use as a spread on sweet breads and muffins or as a seasoning on steaks, chops, fish fillets, poultry, sweet corn, peas, green beans, and other mild-tasting vegetables.

Use oil to extract specific constituents from tarragon or as a medium to preserve the whole herb. You see this in refrigerated or frozen commercial pestos. To make herb oil, mix two packed cups of fresh tarragon with one-third cup oil; any neutral-tasting cooking oil will do. Chop in a food processor or blend in a blender until it has pesto's consistency. Freeze. Use in the same amounts as dried tarragon.

Use tarragon butter or oil within a couple of weeks; moisture in fresh herbs causes the butter or oil to become moldy or rancid (botulinum spores can grow in the mixture). Be sure to freeze any herb mixture you are not using right away. Freezing extends the oil's or butter's usefulness for a couple months.

Cooking

Tarragon is one of the best culinary herbs, especially when fresh. It is a dominant herb, but its flavor melds with many combinations of herbs and vegetables. Explained below are the many ways we use tarragon, based on years of experience. Keep in mind using herbs in cooking is personal, an art developed by experimenting with varying amounts. Recommending specific quantities in recipes can be tricky, so we suggest trying small amounts first. Then taste, and add more herbs until you create a harmonious blend you, and others, find delightful.

One use for tarragon is in a *bouquet garni*, a combination of herbs tied together at the stems or placed in a porous bag. Add a *bouquet garni* to your cooking pot with other ingredients, then remove before serving. A classic *bouquet garni* consists of bay, parsley, thyme, and tarragon that you use in beef stews and vegetable soups. We add the *bouquet garni* to the stew or soup for the last 20 to 25 minutes of cooking.

Another mixture is called *fines herbes*, which has many uses. The classic *fines herbes* is parsley, thyme, chervil, and tarragon, all finely chopped and mixed. Add this mixture to a dish in the last minute of cooking or just before serving. *Fines herbes* is used in sauces, soups, vegetables, egg dishes, sandwich spreads, or with cottage cheese. Keep a small bowl of *fines herbes* on the table so you and your guests can add flavor to particular dishes.

We use three other tarragon combinations. One is half purple ruffles basil and half tarragon, both roughly chopped. We serve this on lettuce salads, melon balls, or fruit salads. A second combination of 1 part spearmint to 3 parts tarragon is absolutely wonderful on melon balls. This we serve in small blue Japanese rice bowls as a dessert, garnished with fresh spearmint. A third combination is tarragon with onion chives. This is good on vegetable salads and egg dishes. Keep in mind that tarragon alone is tasty in all the dishes mentioned.

Below are tarragon recipes you can try. Remember to use tarragon and other herbs to suit your fancy–for decoration, accent, flavor, aroma, and harmony. tarragon and all culinary herbs are a nutritious addition to your fare.

❧Tarragon Melon Balls❧

Serves 15 to 20

1 12 to 15 pound watermelon
1 4 to 5 pound cantaloupe
1 4 to 5 pound honeydew
3 tablespoons fresh French tarragon leaves
2 tablespoons fresh purple ruffles basil leaves
2 sprigs of tarragon for garnish
2 sprigs of basil for garnish

Make melon balls, removing seeds. (Seedless watermelons, if you can get them, save considerable time.) Or you may cut melons into ¾-inch cubes. Using a scissors, chop or snip the tarragon and basil into ⅛-inch strips. Mix with melon balls. Place in refrigerator to chill and to diffuse the herb flavor through the melons.

Just before serving, add tarragon and basil garnish. Substitute spearmint for basil, if you so desire, but reduce the tarragon to ⅓ the amount listed.

❧Tarragon Cheese Sauce❧

Makes 4 dishes

2 tablespoons butter
2 tablespoons flour
1 cup milk
1 cup grated Monterey Jack cheese
2 tablespoons chopped fresh French tarragon

Melt butter in a small saucepan over low heat. Add flour when butter is melted and mix until flour and butter are blended. Add milk and turn heat up to medium high. Stir constantly until sauce thickens and begins to bubble. Remove from heat and add cheese and tarragon. Mix until cheese is melted.

Use this sauce over fish fillets, chicken breasts, pasta, and such vegetables as asparagus, green beans, and carrots. We like to garnish this type of dish with a small piece of tarragon.

❧Fruit Sauce❧

4 servings

1 cup sour cream
3 tablespoons maple syrup
3 tablespoons chopped tarragon
Combine ingredients and add to any number of fruit
    combinations.

TRY THE FOLLOWING:
1 large apple, chopped into ½-inch cubes
1 banana sliced
⅓ cup walnuts or pecans
2 stalks celery, chopped

Mix ingredients with fruit sauce and garnish with a sprig of tarragon. Other herbs that work with the sour cream-maple syrup sauce are spearmint, cilantro, and purple ruffles basil.

❧Melon Patch Tartar Sauce❧

4 servings

1 cup mayonnaise
1 tablespoon chopped sweet pickle
1 tablespoon fresh French tarragon, chopped
1 tablespoon freshly chopped parsley or chervil
1 tablespoon honey or maple syrup
salt and pepper

Mix ingredients and add salt and pepper to taste. This tartar sauce is delicious with any fish or battered-and-fried shellfish. It is also good with poached fish fillets.

Use herbs sparingly at first. Add them gradually until they please your taste buds.

❧ *Bearnaise Sauce* ❧
4 servings

¾ cup white wine
2 tablespoons tarragon vinegar
2 tablespoons finely chopped onion
1 teaspoon finely chopped parsley
1 tablespoon chopped fresh tarragon
2 crushed peppercorns
3 egg yolks
1 cup clarified butter

Mix wine, vinegar, onion, tarragon, parsley, and peppercorns in a small saucepan. Boil until mixture is reduced to one-third. Cool, and strain. Mix egg yolks together in the top of a double boiler and place over simmering water. Add the cooled vinegar-and-wine mixture, stirring all the time. Add the clarified butter, stirring constantly until the sauce has thickened. (Clarified butter: Heat butter in a small saucepan over low heat until melted. Let settle. Pour off the oily liquid–the clarified butter–and discard the curdy, milky substance that has settled to the bottom.)

Bearnaise sauce is great on fish, broiled red meats, and egg dishes.

❧ *Hollandaise Sauce* ❧
4 servings

½ cup clarified butter
4 egg yolks, slightly beaten
2 teaspoons lemon juice
2 tablespoons finely chopped French tarragon

Place egg yolks in the top of double boiler over hot, not boiling, water. Pour clarified butter slowly into the egg yolks, stirring constantly until sauce is mixed and all the butter has been added. Keep beating the mixture until thick. Remove mixture from heat and beat another 2 minutes. Add lemon juice and tarragon. Salt and pepper to taste, return to heat, and beat for 2 minutes more. Use with cooked vegetables (asparagus is great) or broiled or roasted meats.

❧ Creamy Tarragon-Garlic Dip ❧

Serves 8

1 carton (8 ounces) plain yogurt
½ cup dairy sour cream
2 small cloves garlic, crushed
2 tablespoons each fresh parsley and chives, finely chopped
2 to 3 tablespoons fresh French tarragon, finely chopped
1 teaspoon Dijon-style prepared mustard
⅛ teaspoon pepper

Combine all ingredients in medium-sized bowl. Mix well. Cover and chill 2 hours to allow flavors to blend. Serve with assorted raw vegetable dippers. *(Contributed by the American Dairy Association.)*

❧ Sliced Beet and Cucumber Salad ❧

with Creamy Herb Dressing

5 medium-sized unpared beets with tops trimmed
2 medium-sized cucumbers, pared
Boston or Bibb lettuce

DRESSING:

¾ cup dairy sour cream

1 tablespoon tarragon wine vinegar

1 tablespoon prepared horseradish

1 tablespoon sugar

1 tablespoon each fresh chopped tarragon, dill, and chives

1 clove garlic, crushed

½ teaspoon salt

¼ teaspoon pepper

½ cup (2 ounces) crumbled bleu cheese

fresh herbs for garnish

Cover beets with water in large saucepan and bring to boil. Cover and simmer until tender, about 35 minutes. Drain. Place beets in cold water. Slip off skins and remove root ends. Cut beets and cucumbers into ¼-inch thick slices. Arrange them in overlapping rows on a lettuce-lined platter.

Dressing: Combine all ingredients except cheese. Mix well. Spoon dressing over beets and cucumbers. Sprinkle with bleu cheese. Garnish with fresh herbs. *(Contributed by the American Dairy Association.)*

❧ *Poached Turkey Tenderloins* ❧
with Tarragon Sauce

1 to 1½ pounds turkey tenderloins

¾ cup white wine

½ cup celery, chopped

¼ cup green onions, sliced

½ teaspoon salt

¼ teaspoon white pepper

3 tablespoons fresh French tarragon, chopped, or 1 teaspoon dry, crushed

water

In a large skillet, arrange tenderloins in one layer. Add wine, celery, onion, spices, and enough water to cover meat. Cover skillet and poach over low heat about 40 minutes or until no longer pink in the center. Remove tenderloins, reserving the poaching liquid for the tarragon sauce.

SAUCE:
Makes 2 cups
Reserved poaching liquid
3 tablespoons cold water
2 tablespoons cornstarch
3 tablespoons fresh French tarragon, chopped, or ½ teaspoon dry, crushed
1 tablespoon fresh parsley, chopped
1 tablespoon lemon juice
½ cup plain low-fat yogurt

In a saucepan over high heat, bring reserved poaching liquid to boil for 5–10 minutes, to reduce liquid. Strain. Measure 2 cups liquid and return it to saucepan. Bring to boil. Combine cold water and corn starch. Stir into boiling liquid. Reduce heat and add tarragon. Over low heat, cook sauce until slightly thickened. Stir in parsley, lemon juice, and yogurt.

Slice tenderloins into ½-inch medallions. To serve, arrange medallions on steamed spinach. Drizzle with sauce. Garnish with a strip of lemon, if desired. *(Contributed by the Minnesota Turkey Research and Promotion Council, and the National Turkey Federation.)*

MINT
Mentha

Mint

There is a universal appeal to the stimulating, yet comforting, taste and smell of mint. The cool refreshing taste of iced mint tea on a hot summer day is one of life's pleasures. (The sensation of cold in your mouth comes from menthol.) And on a wintry evening, the warm fragrance of hot mint tea is equally nice.

Myth has it that the jealous Persephone changed the nymph Minthe into a low growing plant. Her lover Pluto could not reverse the spell, but with his powers he decreed that the more that Minthe was tread upon, the sweeter she would smell. The wonderful fragrances of peppermint and spearmint have made them popular through the ages as strewing herbs. Mint leaves strewn in dank medieval castles no doubt provided a welcome smell. Scrubbing a table with mint leaves before a meal has long been a tradition. Mint, which is used in some massage oils, is generally considered a symbol of hospitality.

Spearmint, *Mentha spicata*, is a mild mint often used in cooking, and candy's peppermint flavor is widely known. In the eighteenth century peppermint, *Mentha x piperita*, became known as a medicinal herb. Its carminative qualities help indigestion and flatulence. It has also been used for headaches, fevers, insomnia, flu, and colds. Menthol, the most active of the mint-derived substances, comes from peppermint and is said to promote digestion by stimulating the flow of bile to the stomach. Menthol is considered anti-bacterial and anti-parasitic, and is also said to heal ulcers.

Growing

Mints, native to Europe and Asia, are found in all temperate areas, most often in moist places. They grow 24 to 48 inches tall and have pink, white, or purple flowers in July and August. Mints are square-stemmed, with opposite leaves in pairs. Mint leaves vary from light green, wrinkled, and toothed, to dark green, smooth, and slightly hairy. The stems can range from a light green to an almost purplish dark red.

These perennials are easy to grow, but not so easy to identify. Experts maintain there are 25 species, but inter-breeding has produced hundreds of plants. Therefore, taste a plant to get the one you want. You can grow mint from seed, but inter-breeding makes it impossible to get a specific mint. We propagate mint from cuttings at any time or by division in fall.

Plant mint in a moist spot or keep it well watered. Add fertilizer or compost in the fall. If you grow a half hardy mint, mulch it well in November. Mint spreads vigorously, new growth coming from runners or stolons. If you use mint for ground cover, mow it just as it comes into flower. Mint is invasive, so consider sinking a metal or wooden barrier 10 inches in the ground to contain it. We contain the mint growing against our house foundation by constantly mowing the lawn just beyond the mint border. Mint makes an aromatic window box. To control root growth, put individual plants in coffee cans in the box.

Peppermint, *Mentha piperita*, does not produce seed. It is a sterile hybrid, a cross between *Mentha spicata* and *Mentha aquatica*. Some call the different peppermints white and black; they range in color from light green to reddish-purple.

Japanese mint, *Mentha arvensis var piperescens*, is said to be the only true mint in the United States. It is a source of much pharmaceutical menthol throughout the world. Sometimes called Poleo mint, it flowers in the axils of upper leaves, not in terminal spikes like other mints.

Pennyroyal, *Mentha pulegium*, is a half-hardy mint that stays prostrate. It forms an ideal ground cover if kept moist. Pennyroyal grows in full sun to partial shade, like most mints. We use it only as a bug repellent by rubbing leaves on our skin.

Applemint, *Mentha suavolens*, makes a good garnish, as does its smaller cultivar, pineapple mint, Mentha suavolens var variegata. As indicated by the name, it has variegated leaves.

The tiny round leaves of Corsican mint, *Mentha requienii*, make a nice ground cover for a shady area. However, the plant is not very hardy. Corsican mint was once the main flavoring for creme de menthe.

Propagating

Because the seeds of these mints do not reproduce true to the species, they are better propagated by cuttings, divisions, stolons (underground runners of rhizomes that are the mint's methods of spreading through the ground). Use the same cutting/division techniques already described. When you dig up a mint plant, you will see the stolons spreading out from the plant. Cut them into two to three-inch pieces and plant one per 4-inch pot, one inch deep in Cornell mix, wet the mix, and in 7 to 10 days there will be new stems and leaves.

Harvesting

Just cut the plants off right at the ground; they regenerate from the root. Both spearmint and peppermint are very invasive as their stolons spread into adjacent areas, so plant them where they will not get in your way or contain them with an edging that is at least ten inches deep. Harvest mint any time, but young leaves have a better taste. Old leaves may become tough or slightly bitter.

Preserving

Dried mint holds its flavor very well, but fresh mint tastes better. See Chapter 2 for more information on air-drying techniques. Most of us have enjoyed wonderful mint jelly, and mint can also be frozen in oil or made into vinegar.

Cooking

Mint is one of the oldest, most versatile culinary herbs of the Mediterranean area. Two classic combinations are mint with peas and lamb, sometimes served with mint sauce, and mint jelly made using spearmint. Mint leaves tucked into the skin of a lamb roast, along with garlic cloves, enhance the aroma and taste. Mint sauces and relishes are good with summer vegetables such as zucchini, carrots, and sweet corn. Try mint with new potatoes, potato salad, or parsnips. Middle Eastern cracked wheat salad is wonderful with mint. In fact, fresh mint leaves are a refreshing addition to most fruit salads and green salads. It is also fun making peppermint syrup or a lovely peppermint sorbet or sherbet.

Iced and hot mint teas are classics, for their taste and medicinal qualities. Either steep and chill mint tea to make iced tea, or add 1 cup of chopped mint leaves to ½ gallon of water. Chill for several hours and strain before serving over ice. Mint water is truly refreshing on hot summer days.

As a garnish, mint is without peer. A whorl of mint leaves in a glass of iced tea allows you to inhale the peppermint fragrance before tasting the tea. And sprigs of fresh mint leaves are lovely surrounding a roasted leg of lamb.

Before proceeding to the mint recipes, consider one more use for mint. For a refreshing treat, add mint water to your bath or hang a bag full of mint leaves under the faucet as you fill the tub.

Whether you enjoy cooking with mint, taking a tea medicinally, or just walking barefoot through a mint bed on a summer day, you will probably agree with the 16th century herbalist Gerard: *"...The smell rejoiceth the heart of man..."*

❦Mint Julep❦

A nice touch on a hot summer day.

Crush 4 fresh spearmint leaves (preferably of the Kentucky colonel variety) with 1 teaspoon sugar. Place in a tall frosted glass. Fill with crushed ice. Add 1½ ounces Kentucky straight bourbon. Stir. Garnish with fresh spearmint leaves. Enjoy!

❦Refreshing Mint Dressing❦

¼ cup rice or white wine vinegar
1 tablespoon vegetable oil
2 tablespoons snipped fresh mint leaves
½ to 1 teaspoon sugar

Combine ingredients. Whisk before serving. *(Contributed by the Beef Industry Council.)*

❦Mint Sauce❦

2 tablespoons fresh spearmint, chopped
1 teaspoon honey (or 1 teaspoon sugar)
2 tablespoons white wine vinegar
1 tablespoon lemon juice

Using mortar and pestle, grind mint to a paste. Gradually blend in honey, lemon juice, and vinegar. Stir in about ¼ cup boiling water.

This sauce is wonderful when chilled and served with roast lamb. You can also spread it on a leg of lamb in the final minutes of roasting.

❦ Minted Summer Squash ❦

Makes 6 cups

1 cup half-and-half
½ cup packed fresh mint leaves
¼ cup (½ stick) butter
¾ cup sliced green onions
½ cup shredded carrot
1 clove garlic, minced
5 cups sliced mixed summer squash (patty pan, yellow, and
    zucchini)
3 cups condensed chicken broth
Salt and pepper to taste

Combine half-and-half with mint in blender container. Cover and puree until smooth. Set aside. Melt butter in large saucepan. Saute onions, carrot, and garlic until tender (about 5 minutes). Add squash and broth. Heat to boiling. Cover and simmer 10 to 12 minutes, until squash is tender. Puree squash mixture in blender, one third at a time. Return puree to saucepan. Season. Heat through, but do not boil. Stir in reserved cream mixture. Serve immediately. *(Contributed by the American Dairy Association.)*

❦ Bulgur Wheat Salad ❦ with Mint and Parsley

4 to 5 Servings

There are several variations of Middle Eastern salads combining cracked bulgur wheat with mint and parsley. The following is one we like.

¾ cup bulgur wheat
1½ cups boiling water
1 tablespoon olive oil
2 tablespoons lemon juice
2 tablespoons fresh mint, chopped

4 tablespoons fresh parsley, chopped
4 tablespoons mild onion, chopped
2 tomatoes, chopped
salt and freshly-ground pepper
4 to 5 lettuce leaves, preferably Bibb
fresh branch of mint and lemon slices for garnish

Place bulgur wheat in a bowl and cover with boiling water. Allow to sit until all water has been absorbed and the wheat is swollen (about 15 minutes). Add the mint, parsley, oil, onion, lemon juice, and tomatoes. Mix gently. Add salt and pepper. Spoon the salad onto lettuce-covered individual serving plates. Garnish with mint and lemon slices.

❧ Fresh Green Pea Soup with Mint ❧

Try this soup in late June when you have a nice batch of peas to shell.

3 cups shelled peas
1¼ cups half-and-half
1¼ cups chicken bouillon
freshly ground black pepper and salt to taste
2 tablespoons finely chopped mint

Gently cook shelled peas in lightly salted water. Blend until smooth in blender along with the chicken bouillon and half-and-half. Season to taste. Stir in the chopped mint and briefly reheat to serve.

This also makes a lovely chilled soup. Wait to add mint until just before serving. Do not forget to garnish each bowl with a branch of fresh mint.

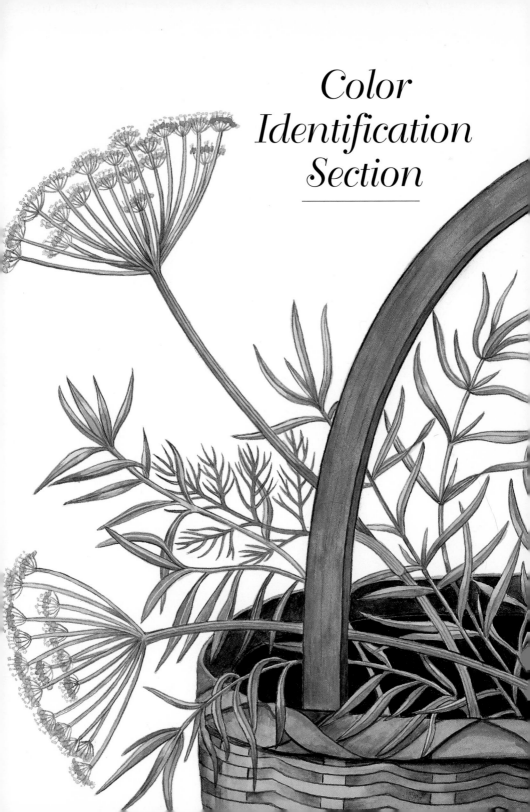

*Color
Identification
Section*

BASIL
Ocimum basilicum

93

CHIVES
Allium schoenoprasum

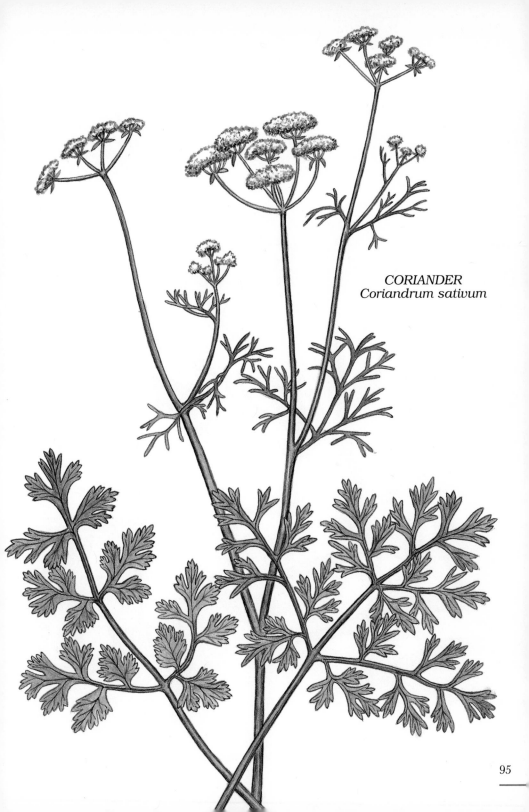

CORIANDER
Coriandrum sativum

DAY LILY
Hermerocallis fulva

JOHNY JUMP UP
Viola kitaibeliana

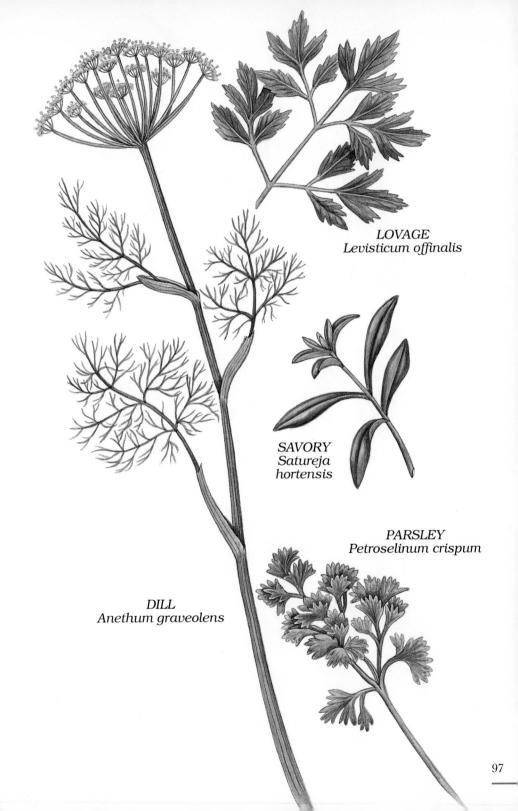

LOVAGE
Levisticum offinalis

SAVORY
*Satureja
hortensis*

PARSLEY
Petroselinum crispum

DILL
Anethum graveolens

FRENCH TARRAGON
Artemisin drancunculus

MINT
Mentha

OREGANO
Origanum vulgare

ROSEMARY
Rosmarinus officinalis

101

SAGE
Salvia officinalis

102

THYME
Thymus vulgaris

103

Herb	Latin Name	Annual	Perennial	Biennial	Plant Height	Days to Germination
Anise Hyssop	*Agastache foeniculum*	X	X		1.5-3 ft.	14 days
Basil	*Ocimum basilicum*	X			1-2 ft.	5-10 days
Bay Laurel	*Laurus nobilis*		X		4-5 ft.	40 days to 6 months
Borage	*Borago officinalis*	X			2-3 ft.	7-14 days
Chamomile	*Matricaria recutita*	X			1.5-2 ft.	10-14 days
Chervil	*Anthriscus cerefolium*	X			1-2 ft.	14-21 days
Chives	*Allium schoenoprasum*		X		1-1.5 ft.	10 days
Coriander	*Coriandrum sativum*	X			1-3 ft.	7-10 days
Dill	*Anethum graveolens*	X			2-3 ft.	14 days
Fennel	*Foeniculum vulgare*		X		3-4 ft.	6 days
French Tarragon	*Artemisia dracunculus sativa*		X		2 ft.	Vegetatively Propagated
Garlic	*Allium sativum*		X		2 ft.	Bulb Propagated
Horseradish	*Amoracia rusticana*		X		3 ft.	Vegetatively Propagated
Lemon Balm	*Melissa officinalis*		X		1.5 - 2 ft.	7-14 days
Lovage	*Levisticum offinalis*		X		2.5-6 ft.	8-10 days
Marjoram	*Origanum majorana*		X		1-2 ft.	14 days
Mint, peppermint	*Mentha piperita*		X		2 ft.	Vegetatively Propagated
Mint, spearmint	*Mentha spicata*		X		2 ft.	Vegetatively Propagated
Mint, orange	*Mentha x piperta varicitrata*		X		2 ft.	Vegetatively Propagated
Oregano	*Origanum vulgare hirtum*		X		1-2 ft.	14 days
Parsley	*Petroselinum crispum*			X	10-18 in.	21 days
Rosemary	*Rosmarinus officinalis*		X		2-6 ft.	14-21 days
Sage	*Salvia officinalis*		X		1-2 ft.	7-10 days
Savory	*Satureja hortensis*	X			8-10 in.	5 days
Shallot	*Allium cepa*		X		1 ft.	Bulb Propagated
Sorrel	*Rumex acetosa*		X		2 ft.	7-10 days
Thyme	*Thymus vulgaris*		X		6-15 in.	4-5 days

Chart

Full Sun	Part Sun	Shade	Uses	Page No.
X	X		stuffing, soups, salads, desserts, tea	185
X			lamb, fish, poultry, beans, pasta, salads, tomatoes, eggs, cheese dishes	35
X	X		stews, sauces, soups	151
X			vegetables, salads, garnish for drinks, desserts, pastry, or candied	186
	X		potpourri, teas	178
X	X	X	vegetables, soups, meats, cheeses	153
X			egg dishes, fish, vegetables	51
X	X		stews, vegetables, tomato sauces, meat, poultry	61
X			vegetables, fish, pork, pickles	155
X			breads, sausage, apple pie, eggs, fish, soups	157
X	X		fruits, cheese dishes, poultry, vegetables, eggs	71
X			soups, salads, creamed vegetables, sour cream, spreads	158
X			roast beef, cole slaw, cream cheese	161
X	X	X	fruits, custards, egg dishes,white sauce for fish	180
X	X	X	soups, salads, stews	162
X			poultry, lamb, beef, fish, vegetables	172
X	X		candies, chocolates, liquers	83
X	X		drinks, salads, vegetables	83
X	X		salads, drinks	83
X			tomato sauces, salads	109
X	X		salads, egg dishes, soups, potatoes	165
X	X		veal, lamb, vegetables, herb butters	123
X			stuffing, soups, sauces, vegetables, egg dishes	135
X			beans, poultry	169
X			vegetables, egg dishes, salads, casseroles	170
X	X		chicken, eggs, soup	171
X	X		meats, vegetables, salads	145

OREGANO
Origanum vulgare

CHAPTER 9

Oregano

You may be surprised to learn that oregano is a flavor rather than a specific plant. The plant most people call oregano is actually wild marjoram. Anyone who loves the aromatic pleasure of pizza and spaghetti knows oregano is for cooking, although centuries ago the primary use was medicinal. The flavor, which is hot and peppery, can also be described as strong and spicy.

Rather than just one oregano, there is a whole genus and their flavor varies from mild to very strong. For example, *Origanum onites,* also called pot marjoram, is much stronger than its cousin, sweet marjoram. Many of the oreganos contain the same essential oil, dominated by carvacrol, which gives oregano its fragrance. We grow *Origanum hirtum,* also known as *Origanum heracleoticum.* Our understanding is the hills of Greece are full of the common oregano, *Origanum,* which grows wild. The word *Origanum* comes from two Greek words meaning joy and mountain. A crown of oregano, for weddings or other special occasions, supposedly brings joy.

Growing

Oregano grows best in full sun in sandy, well drained soil, but it tolerates a variety of circumstances. As with most herbs, it is a forgiving plant and wants to get along with you. The flavor, though, is better if it is grown in full sun versus semi-shade.

Most oreganos grow 1 to 2 feet tall and sprawl as they grow. They are usually vigorous and hardy as far north as Zone 4, particularly if you mulch them in late fall. They are perennials with square mint-like stems.

Flowers vary in color from white to rosy-pink to purple. The white-flowered plants often have the best flavor, while the rosy-pink and purple flowers are nice in dried flower bouquets. Oregano blossoms July to September in the North.

Propagating

To buy oregano plants, ask the grower if you can taste them to be sure you get the species you want. However, before nibbling the leaves, ask about any chemicals that were used.

Oregano can easily be grown from seed, but because there is so much variation, we prefer to propagate it through cuttings or by digging root divisions in the spring. If you choose to grow your oregano from seed, it will germinate in about four days at 70°F, uncovered in light. Once you have the plants established, you can choose the ones with good flavor, and discard the rest.

Harvesting

Harvest oregano any time after the plant reaches a height of about 6 inches. Keep in mind, however, the flavor is stronger when the plant is flowering.

If you plant new oregano plants, they probably will not be ready to harvest until late July. With an established bed of perennial oregano, your first harvest will be in June. It should continue growing enough to harvest again in July and August. After that, let it grow to strengthen it for winter.

When we want 2 or 3 tablespoons of fresh oregano for a summer dish, we pinch off the top few inches of the oregano plant with our fingers. The leaves and stems of this soft, tender growth can be chopped and used.

To dry oregano for later use, go down to the woody stem, cutting about the top half, to hang in bunches. It dries very easily. Store the whole branch until you are ready to use it; this will preserve more flavor. When you are ready to use it, strip the dried leaves from the stem, and crumble them. Discard the stem.

Preserving

Properly dried, oregano maintains its full and hot flavor for a long time. You can also freeze it in oil. But, of course, we prefer the taste of fresh oregano.

Cooking

Oregano is a dominant herb, so we use it in small quantities on pizza, spaghetti, and tomatoes. We also enjoy fresh or dried oregano with poultry and beef, in breads, and in egg and cheese dishes.

❧ Greek Salad with Fresh Oregano ❧

4 Servings

equal parts olive oil and white vinegar
black pepper, freshly-ground
3 tablespoons fresh oregano leaves, chopped
2 cloves garlic, minced
1 onion, sliced
salt, a pinch
5 tomatoes, sliced
15 whole, pitted Greek black olives
2 cucumbers, sliced
1 cup feta cheese, crumbled
½ cup parsley, chopped

This recipe has wonderful full flavor and is a particular favorite of ours. The sight and smell of the marinade is a great appetite stimulant.

We always marinate on the butcher block in a lovely Japanese bowl, using chopsticks to stir.

Combine oil, vinegar, and pepper. Gently stir in the onion, garlic, oregano, and salt. Keep the mixture at room temperature for 2 hours, stirring occasionally. Just before serving add tomatoes, cucumbers, and olives to marinade. Top each serving with crumbled feta cheese and chopped parsley.

Turkey Wild Rice Meatballs

6 Servings

This is a low fat, high carbohydrate version of an Italian favorite.

MEATBALLS:
1¼ pounds lean ground turkey
1 cup cooked wild rice
¼ cup beef broth (from 15-ounce can)
1 egg, beaten
¼ cup chopped green onions
1 garlic clove, minced
¼ teaspoon salt
⅛ teaspoon pepper
2 tablespoons oil

SAUCE:
1¾ cups (or remaining) beef broth
1 6-ounce can tomato paste
1 can (4¼ ounces) sliced mushrooms, undrained
½ cup chopped green pepper
½ cup sliced black olives
¼ cup chopped onion
2 tablespoons chopped fresh parsley
2 tablespoons chopped fresh oregano leaves

Mix meatball ingredients. Shape in 1-inch balls and brown in 2 tablespoons of oil over medium heat. Move to side of pan. Add sauce ingredients, blending carefully. Stir sauce and meatballs together. Simmer, covered, 30 minutes or until sauce is thickened and vegetables tender. Meanwhile, prepare 6 ounces of spaghetti as directed on package. Serve meatballs over spaghetti. *(Contributed by Minnesota Paddy Wild Rice Council.)*

Potato Salad on a Stick

Serves 8

An oregano vinaigrette is tasty with any potato salad.

4 medium red potatoes (6 to 7 ounces)
1 medium red bell pepper, seeded and cut into 1½-inch squares
1 medium onion, cut into wedges
1 medium cucumber, cut into chunks
16 cherry tomatoes
8 ounces salami, cut into cubes
4 ounces feta cheese, crumbled
oregano vinaigrette (recipe follows)

Cook potatoes in covered saucepan until tender (35 to 45 minutes). Drain and cool slightly. Cut into 1½-inch chunks. In large bowl, combine potatoes with remaining ingredients. Add vinaigrette, toss, and coat. Marinate at room temperature 1 hour. Spear marinated ingredients with eight bamboo skewers, dividing equally. Arrange on serving plates. Sprinkle with cheese.

Oregano vinaigrette: Combine ⅓ cup olive oil, 3 tablespoons red wine vinegar, 1 medium garlic clove (chopped), and 1½ teaspoon dried oregano. Whisk to blend, mix in salt and pepper to taste. Serves eight. *(Contributed by Red River Valley Potato Growers Association.)*

Easy Microwave Turkey Lasagna

Serves 8

1 pound ground turkey, defrosted
1 clove garlic, chopped
1 cup onions, chopped
1 can (14½-ounces) tomatoes chopped, reserve liquid
1 6-ounce can tomato paste
2½ teaspoons Italian seasoning or oregano
8 uncooked lasagna noodles
1 12-ounce carton low fat cottage cheese
2 cups shredded skim mozzarella cheese (8 ounces)

In a 2-quart, microwave-safe casserole dish, combine ground turkey, garlic, and onion. Cover and microwave at 100% power (high) for 5 minutes, stirring halfway through cooking time. Stir in tomatoes, including juice, tomato paste, and seasoning. Microwave, uncovered, at 100% power for 5 minutes. Lightly grease 2-quart oblong microwave-safe casserole dish. Spoon ⅓ of sauce (about 1⅓ cup) over bottom of dish. Top with 4 lasagna noodles, breaking them to fit. Spoon cottage cheese over noodles. Sprinkle mozzarella over top of cottage cheese. Spoon ⅓ more of sauce over cheese. Top with remaining noodles. Spoon remaining sauce over noodles and cover with vented plastic wrap. Place several layers of paper towels on bottom of microwave oven to absorb any spillovers. Microwave at 100% power for 5 minutes. Reduce power to 50% (medium) and microwave 20 to 25 minutes or until noodles are tender. *(Contributed by National Turkey Federation.)*

❧Grilled Sirloin Steak with❧ Red Onion Kabobs

4 Servings

1¼ pounds boneless beef sirloin steak, cut 1-inch thick

¼ cup red wine vinegar

3 tablespoons olive oil

2 teaspoons dried oregano leaves or 6 teaspoons fresh leaves, divided

1 teaspoon honey

¾ teaspoon cracked black pepper, divided

½ teaspoon each dry mustard and salt

1 medium red onion, cut into 8 wedges

Combine vinegar, oil, 1½ teaspoons dried oregano (or 4½ teaspoons fresh), honey, ¼ teaspoon pepper, mustard, and salt. Place onion wedges in plastic bag. Add marinade, turning to coat. Close bag securely and marinate while preparing coals. Meanwhile, soak 8 6-inch bamboo skewers in water 10 minutes. Combine remaining oregano and black pepper. Press herb mixture evenly into both sides of steak. Remove onions from marinade. Reserve marinade. Skewer onion wedges in two places through all layers, using 2 wedges for each kabob. Place steak and kabobs on grill over coals, turning steak and kabobs once. Brush with reserved marinade occasionally. Broil steak about 16 minutes for rare, 20 minutes for medium. Preparation time: 10 minutes. Marinating time: 30 minutes. Cooking time: 16 to 20 minutes.

Mexican Beef Stir-fry

4 Servings

1 pound beef flank steak
2 tablespoons vegetable oil
1 teaspoon each ground cumin and dried oregano leaves
1 clove garlic, minced
1 red bell pepper, cut into strips
1 medium onion, cut into thin wedges
1 to 2 jalapeño peppers*, cut into slivers
3 cups sliced Romaine lettuce, cut ¼ inch

Cut flank steak into ⅛-inch thick strips. Combine oil, cumin, oregano, and garlic. Reserve half. Heat half the seasoned oil in large non-stick frying pan over medium heat until hot. Add red pepper, onion, and jalapeño pepper. Stir-fry 2 to 3 minutes or until crisp-tender. Remove and set aside. In same pan stir-fry beef strips, half at a time, in reserved oil 1 to 2 minutes. Return vegetables to pan and heat through. Serve beef mixture over lettuce. Preparation time: 15 minutes. Cooking time: 8 to 10 minutes.

*Remove interior ribs and seeds if a milder flavor is desired.

❧Beef and Two Pepper Stew❧

4 Servings

1¼ pounds well trimmed beef tip roast, cut into 1-inch pieces
½ cup coarsely chopped onion
1 large clove garlic, minced
1 tablespoon vegetable oil
1½ teaspoons dried oregano leaves
1 teaspoon ground cumin
½ teaspoon each crushed red pepper pods and salt
4 medium tomatoes, chopped and divided
½ cup water
1 can (4 ounces) whole green chilies
1 tablespoon cornstarch
¼ cup sliced green onion tops

Brown beef, onion, and garlic in oil in Dutch oven. Pour off drippings. Combine oregano, cumin, red pepper, and salt. Sprinkle over beef. Add 3 cups tomatoes and water, stirring to combine. Reserve remaining tomato. Cover tightly and simmer 1 hour 55 minutes, or until beef is tender. Meanwhile, drain green chilies, reserving liquid. Cut chilies into ½-inch pieces. Add to beef mixture. Combine cornstarch and reserved liquid. Gradually stir into stew and cook, uncovered, until thickened. Stir in reserved tomato. Garnish with green onion tops.

Chunky Beef Chili

6 servings (1½ cups)

2¼ pounds beef for stew
1 cup each chopped green pepper and coarsely chopped onion
2 cloves garlic, minced
1 teaspoon salt
2 tablespoons oil
1 can (28 ounce) Italian style plum tomatoes, broken up
1 cup water
1 can (6 ounce) tomato paste
3 tablespoons chili powder
1 teaspoon dried oregano leaves
½ teaspoon crushed red pepper pods, if desired
1 can (15½ ounces) kidney beans, drained
6 tablespoons shredded cheddar cheese
condiments: avocado chunks, chopped onion, and dairy sour
       cream

Trim excess fat from beef cubes. Cut each into 2 to 3 pieces. Brown beef, green pepper, onion, and garlic in oil in large frying pan or Dutch oven. Pour off drippings. Sprinkle salt over beef. Add tomatoes, water, tomato paste, chili powder, oregano, and crushed red pepper, if desired. Cover tightly and cook slowly 1½ hours or until beef is tender. Add beans and continue cooking, uncovered, 20 to 30 minutes. Sprinkle each serving with cheese. Garnish with selected condiments. Preparation time: 20 minutes Cooking time: 2 hours, 10 minutes.

❧ Cajun Beef Tenderloin Roast ❧

A beef tenderloin roast yields four 3-ounce cooked servings per pound

3 to 3½-pound beef tenderloin roast
1 teaspoon each dried oregano leaves, dried thyme leaves,
    paprika, and salt
½ teaspoon each freshly ground black pepper, garlic powder,
    onion powder, and ground white pepper
¼ teaspoon ground red pepper
lemon slices, if desired
celery leaves, if desired

Combine oregano, thyme, paprika, salt, black pepper, garlic powder, onion powder, white pepper, and red pepper. Rub over surface of beef tenderloin roast. Place roast on rack in open roasting pan. Insert roast meat thermometer so bulb is centered in thickest part. Do not add water. Do not cover. Roast in 425° (hot) oven to rare. Allow approximately 45 to 50 minutes. Remove the roast when the meat thermometer registers 135° for rare. Allow the roast to stand for15 minutes in a warm place before carving. Roast temperatures will continue to rise to reach 140°. Preparation time: 10 minutes. Cooking time: 45 to 50 minutes.

Greek Style Beef in Pita

2 to 3 Servings

8-12 ounces boneless beef chuck top blade steak

2 tablespoons olive oil, divided

1 tablespoons lemon juice

1 clove garlic, minced

¾ teaspoon dried oregano leaves

½ teaspoon salt

2 to 3 halves pita bread

¼ cup each plain low fat yogurt

¼ cup seeded chopped tomato

1 small green pepper, cut into strips

1 small onion, cut into lengthwise slices

Partially freeze beef blade steak to firm; slice across the grain into ¼-inch strips. Combine 1 tablespoon oil, lemon juice, garlic, oregano, and salt. Add meat, turning to coat. Wrap pita bread in foil and heat in 350° oven 5 to 7 minutes or until warm. Meanwhile, combine yogurt and tomato. Reserve. Heat large frying pan over medium heat. Add steak strips and stir-fry until browned. Do not overcook. Remove from pan. Reserve. Add remaining oil and green pepper to frying pan and cook 3 minutes, stirring occasionally. Stir in onion and cook 2 minutes. Add beef and heat through. Serve in warmed pita bread. Top with yogurt and tomato sauce. Preparation time: 10 to 15 minutes. Cooking time: 8 to 10 minutes. Freezing time: 15 minutes.

❧Hot and Spicy Microwave Beef Barbecue❧

4 Servings

1 pound beef top round steak, cut ¾-inch thick
1 medium onion, thinly sliced and separated into rings
¾ cup original flavor barbecue sauce
2 teaspoons chili powder
½ teaspoon dried oregano leaves
4 corn muffins, quartered

Slice steak into ⅛-inch thick strips. Spread beef strips in layer over bottom of microwave-safe baking dish (11¾- by 7½-inch). Layer onions over beef. Cover with waxed paper and microwave at 50% power (approximately 325 watts) for 7 minutes, stirring once. Combine barbecue sauce, chili powder, and oregano. Stir into beef mixture and continue cooking, covered at medium 10 to 12 minutes, stirring once. Arrange muffins on individual plates. Top with an equal amount of beef mixture.

ROSEMARY
Rosmarinus officinalis

Rosemary

An attractive plant with lovely blue flowers, rosemary is another herb rich in tradition both as a medicinal and culinary herb. It is a dominant herb with a minty, pine-like scent, which prepares your taste buds for rosemary's sagey, almost minty flavor. Its wonderful fragrance is surely one reason rosemary is entwined with flowers for the traditional bride's wreath. In *Bancke's Herbal* we are told of rosemary: *"Smell it oft and it shall keep thee youngly."* And, of course, there is Shakespeare's famous quote: *"...rosemary, that's for remembrance..."*

Growing

Rosemary is a slow-growing, half-hardy tender perennial. The upper side of the 1-inch needles, set in pairs along the stem, is a deep green while the underside is greyish-white. The small flowers grow in clusters and are usually a lovely pale blue. The plant blossoms between late September and spring in Minnesota, and overwinters indoors.

It comes in two forms, upright and prostrate. Upright rosemary, *Rosemarinus officinalis*, grows upward, making a 1½- to 2-foot shrub. Prostrate rosemary, *Rosemarinus officinalis prostratus*, has a more trailing habit; it is almost like a ground cover with slightly curved branches. The taste and aroma of upright and prostrate rosemary are identical. Use both in a diffuser as a room freshener.

Outdoors, rosemary thrives in full sun. It can tolerate dry conditions, but a sheltered position in well drained soil containing some lime, soil ph of 6.5 to 7.0, is best. It grows vigorously in regions with a more Mediterranean climate.

In the North, rosemary is a tender perennial so you must bring it indoors for winter. It can tolerate light frost, so we let ours take a little fall frost just to kill insects that might be lurking on it before we bring it inside. The only problem we have had with pests on rosemary is mealy bugs and aphids which we have controlled with insecticidal soap.

Indoors, rosemary likes a sunny cool spot, but it does not like to become dried out. We recommend using a porous soil mix and watering when the soil surface is dry.

Propagating

Grow rosemary from seed or propagate from cuttings, layering, or divisions. We do not grow prostrate rosemary from seed because it does not come up true. Rosemary seeds have a poor germination rate, about 20%, and the plants are variable. Seeds germinate in about 10 days in a greenhouse. It is also a very slow-growing seedling, taking about 5 months to get a 4-inch pot from seed. We plant the seeds in drills, with our rows 1 to ½ inch apart. See page 13 for more information on drilling. We then cover the seed lightly with horticultural vermiculite, water the tray, cover with clear plastic, and put it under grow lights at 60°F. After germination starts, in about 10 days, we remove the plastic and keep the soil surface moist by misting the tray twice a day. We transplant the seedlings as soon as they show true leaves. We leave the tray under the lights for 2 months before we give up on it, because there will be no more germination. Be careful not to let rosemary dry out indoors; it is hard to rejuvenate. We mist our indoor rosemary with water at least once a day.

Propagating from cuttings is somewhat easier. Take about a 3-inch stem cutting and strip off half of the leaves before inserting it into a Cornell Peat-Lite soil mix that has been pre-moistened. Water the cuttings and cover them with plastic, being careful not to let it touch the cuttings. The soil temperature should be 70 to 75°F, with air temperature being no higher than 80°F. Cuttings need full light, but do not place them in the sun. You will see roots in 3 to 4 weeks if the cuttings came from a vigorously-growing plant.

The prostratus variety roots much more easily than the upright rosemary. It can also be propagated by layering. See page 11 for more information on layering. The prostratus will send down roots wherever a leaf margin touches the soil.

Harvesting

Harvesting rosemary is simple. Cut a few inches off a branch and harvest the leaves (needles) if you are using them immediately. If drying or freezing them, harvest the branches. We harvest throughout the year, being careful to leave one-fourth of the plant for future growth.

Preserving

Preserve rosemary by freezing or drying. To freeze, rinse the branches in water and let them dry on a towel. Place them in a Ziploc bag without blanching, and place the bag in a freezer. When you're ready to use it, slide your thumb and index finger down the stem to remove the needles.

To dry rosemary, hang a three- or four-sprig bunch inside a cupboard for 10 to 15 days. Remove the dry needles and store them in an airtight jar in a dark place. Some people place rosemary in a brown paper bag in the refrigerator to dry.

We have not stored rosemary powder, but to make powder, grind the needles with a mortar and pestle. Store the powder in an air-tight jar in a dark place.

Cooking

The texture of rosemary's pine-needle-like leaves is semi-hard, and tough. Therefore, mince the leaves for fresh use and make sure they are well cooked. Rosemary is a dominant herb, meaning it may overpower mild-tasting fruits or vegetables. With this in mind, an easy way to use rosemary is to mince the needles very fine (it takes a little patience), then sprinkle them over baking fish or a dish of melon balls. Or, in the case of roasting chicken with rosemary, remove the rosemary branch from the cavity of the bird after roasting and before serving. Follow your recipe for roasting time and oven temperature. After slicing the bird, garnish the platter with a second sprig and perhaps a few garlic chive blossoms or five calendula flowers.

Rosemary is a great accent to such wild game dishes as rabbit, pheasant, or quail. It is one of the few herbs whose essence lasts during long, slow cooking. Remove the branch of rosemary before serving.

Beef and lamb dishes, using cuts or ground meat, do nicely with rosemary's strong, delicious flavor. Veal is also beautifully accented by rosemary, and, as a flavoring in dressing, rosemary is great.

Next time you grill on the barbecue, add a few rosemary branches to the coals for an enjoyable aroma. Use a rosemary branch to brush the meat with a marinade that also contains rosemary.

Rosemary may upstage the delicate flavors in vegetable dishes, so use it lightly. It can nicely accent potato dishes, and the taste is especially agreeable with squash (see recipe below for Grilled Summer Vegetables with Tangy Lemon Butter).

These ideas may inspire you to tie your entire meal to a rosemary theme. You could have rosemary with the above meat and vegetables dishes, served on a table with rosemary scents wafting from a centerpiece diffuser. You could make a wine vinegar with rosemary. Rosemary flour, made by pounding leaves with a mortar and pestle, is a good flavor addition to biscuits. You can serve rosemary tea. As the *Grete Herbal* says, the tea helps *"...weyknesse of ye brayne..."* We add 1 cup of boiling water to 1 tablespoon of fresh rosemary leaves. Cover and let steep for 4 minutes. Strain and serve. Tea balls or cloth tea holders also work well. If you are serving cold tea, consider ice cubes made this way: Put a few rosemary sprigs along with blossoms of Johnny jump-ups and bits of mint into your ice cube trays. Cover with water and freeze. The cubes are beautiful, especially if you use clear water.

Rosemary makes for wonderful traditions. Something about the piney aroma blends perfectly with your Thanksgiving turkey, Hanukkah candles, and Christmas trees. At the holidays you can decorate a live potted rosemary with tiny red ribbons and balls. How about weaving a garland of fresh rosemary to encircle a roasted goose? It is always a welcome touch to tuck fragrant rosemary sprigs into your greeting cards and letters. Rosemary's uses are only restricted by your imagination. These recipes should help you to think creatively.

❧ Cornbread with Rosemary ❧

Delicious with the Nutburger recipe on page 131, and the Greek Salad with Fresh Oregano recipe on page 111.

1 cup all-purpose flour
1 cup cornmeal
2 tablespoons honey
Dash of salt (optional)
¼ cup oil or melted butter
1 cup milk
1 egg, beaten
2½ teaspoons baking powder
1 teaspoon rosemary, minced or ground

Preheat oven to 425°. Grease an 8-inch pan. Sift together flour, cornmeal, salt, and baking powder. Use scissors or sharp knife to mince rosemary needles, or pound using a mortar and pestle. Add to the flour mixture. Stir in honey, oil, milk, and beaten egg. Mix until moistened. Bake 20 minutes or until golden brown. Serve hot with a garnish of fresh rosemary.

❧ Roasted (or Fried) Potatoes with Rosemary ❧

Potatoes are particularly tasty with rosemary.
A nice alternative to the traditional potatoes with sour cream and chives is to
snip fresh rosemary onto the sour cream.

2 large potatoes, peeled and sliced

2 tablespoons chopped rosemary needles

3 tablespoons minced green onion

½ dried cayenne pepper, crushed, or ¼ teaspoon dried cayenne
    pepper

1 tablespoon sunflower seeds (salted, shelled)

1 tablespoon fresh lemon juice

1 tablespoon melted butter

salt and freshly ground pepper, to taste

To Roast: Mix first five ingredients and place in oiled heavy pan or skillet. Squeeze lemon juice and drizzle the butter over mixture. Preheat oven to 400° and roast for 55 minutes or until done. Season lightly with salt and pepper.

To Fry: Place first four ingredients in a skillet along with salt and pepper. Cover and fry over medium heat for 10 minutes. Season again. Stir, adding lemon juice and butter. Sprinkle with sunflower seeds and fry an additional 10 minutes. Serve, garnished with (you guessed it) a sprig of fresh rosemary.

❧ Rosemary Potato Omelet ❧

Easy and delicious, and the flavor is great.

Mix ½ tablespoon finely minced rosemary with 2 cups mashed potatoes. Add 1 tablespoon flour, 1 tablespoon milk, 1 tablespoon oil, and 2 beaten eggs. Salt and pepper to taste. Bake in a greased pie tin at 325° until browned, about 20 minutes.

❧ Shiitake Mushrooms with Rosemary ❧

4 servings

1 pound shiitake mushrooms
4 tablespoons olive oil
1 large garlic clove, minced
1 to 2 teaspoons fresh rosemary, chopped
1 large red bell pepper
1 white or yellow onion
1 cup chicken broth
¼ cup water
1 tablespoon cornstarch
2 to 3 tablespoons fresh parsley, chopped

Remove stems from shiitake caps and slice thin. Slice shiitake caps, pepper, and onions into ¼-inch wide strips. Heat oil in large skillet. Add garlic, rosemary, and sliced shiitake stems. Stir-fry over medium heat for about 3 minutes. Add sliced pepper, onions, and shiitake caps. Continue stir-frying another 3 minutes. Add broth and bring to a boil. Mix cornstarch with ¼ cup water and add to mushroom mixture. Cook until thickened. Serve over egg noodles or rice. Finally, garnish with chopped parsley.

❧ Herb Sauce ❧

1 cup of strained beef poaching liquid (the liquid in which roast beef was cooked)
1½ teaspoons cornstarch
¾ teaspoon snipped rosemary or ¼ teaspoon dried rosemary leaves, crushed
2 dashes pepper
1 teaspoon butter

Place poaching liquid in small saucepan. Combine cornstarch, rosemary, and pepper. Add to liquid and bring to a boil. Stir over high heat until thickened, 1 to 2 minutes. Stir in butter. Yield: approximately 1 cup. *(Contributed by Minnesota Beef Council.)*

❧*Leg of Lamb with Rosemary*❧

Serves 6 to 8

Mint with lamb is the classic combination, but lamb is also wonderful with rosemary and garlic.

1 5-pound leg of lamb
1 clove garlic
1 onion
1 teaspoon black peppercorns, crushed
2 teaspoons grated lemon rind
2 sprigs rosemary plus 1 for garnish
1 cup red wine
salt, to taste

Use the shank of the leg of lamb. You or the butcher should trim much of the fat, leaving about 5 pounds after trimming. If the leg is larger, ask the butcher to cut a few chops for broiling, and perhaps some more for stewing. Preheat oven to 400° and reduce to 325° when you begin roasting. Mince garlic and chop onion, peppercorns, and lemon rind. Combine all with rosemary leaves and ¼ cup wine in a mortar. Use the pestle to grind finely. Make slits at an angle in the leg of lamb. Stuff each slit with the ground mixture. Place whole leg, fat side up, on a rack in an uncovered pan. Bake 35 minutes per pound. After 2 hours, continue baking but baste several times with the remaining ¾ cup wine. Slice and serve with fresh rosemary garnish.

❧ *Chicken Breasts with Rosemary* ❧

4 servings

Rosemary is a wonderful flavor with all chicken dishes.

1 tablespoon fresh rosemary leaves, minced fine
4 chicken breasts, halved, skinned, and boned; pounded to ¼ inch
¼ cup melted butter
¼ cup flour
¼ cup dry white wine
2 tablespoons lemon juice
salt and pepper, to taste

Dredge chicken in flour. Melt butter in heavy skillet and add rosemary. Brown chicken 3 minutes on each side, and continue cooking until tender. Add wine, lemon juice, salt, and pepper. Bring to a boil. Turn down heat and simmer 3 minutes, or until sauce is thickened. Place chicken on serving platter. Spoon sauce over it and garnish with a sprig of fresh rosemary.

❧ *Nutburgers with Rosemary,* ❧ *Thyme, and Oregano*

One of our favorite recipes.

1 large onion, finely chopped
3 sticks celery, diced
¼ pound butter
1 teaspoon each rosemary and oregano, both minced fine
1 teaspoon thyme leaves (or substitute herbs of your choice)
¼ cup whole wheat flour
2 teaspoons vegetable bouillon dissolved in 1¼ cup hot water
1 pound mixed nuts, finely chopped or grated
4½ cups fine whole wheat bread crumbs
2 teaspoons yeast extract
soy sauce, salt, and pepper, to taste

Saute celery and onions in butter over medium heat for 1 minute until clear. Add herbs and flour. Stir and cook for 2 minutes. Stir in the bouillon-water mixture, nuts, all but ¼ cup bread crumbs, and yeast extract. Season with soy sauce, salt, and pepper. Cool mixture thoroughly, then form 8 large patties or 12 smaller ones. Sprinkle liberally with the reserved bread crumbs. If you plan to freeze half the batch, do it at this point. Gently fry the burgers in a little oil. Serve on sliced whole wheat Kaiser rolls with lots of pickles and other condiments. The burgers are delicious and filling. Because the recipe makes 8 large or 12 small patties, we freeze half for a later meal.

❦ Grilled Summer Vegetables with ❦ Tangy Lemon Butter Vegetables

Tangy Lemon Butter is also delicious on grilled fish and poultry.

VEGETABLES:
2 each medium-sized yellow squash and zucchini, trimmed, halved (about 5 ounces each)
1 medium-sized eggplant, sliced ½-inch thick (about 1 pound)
2 red peppers, seeded and quartered
2 yellow peppers, seeded and quartered
3 medium red potatoes, unpared, cooked almost tender, sliced ½-inch thick
6 large green onions
salt and pepper

TANGY LEMON BUTTER:
½ cup clarified butter
2 tablespoons fresh lemon juice
2 teaspoons minced fresh rosemary
1 teaspoon minced fresh thyme
1 teaspoon Dijon-style prepared mustard
1 clove garlic, crushed

For Sauce: Combine all ingredients.

For Vegetables: Score squash, zucchini, and eggplant. Season all vegetables with salt and pepper. Place vegetables directly on grill. Brush butter mixture generously over vegetables. Grill over hot coals until vegetables are tender, 5 to 6 minutes on each side, basting occasionally. Serve vegetables warm or at room temperature. *(Contributed by The American Dairy Association.)*

SAGE
Salvia officinalis

CHAPTER 11

Sage

Most of us associate sage with poultry dressing or pork sausage. It is commonly sold as rubbed sage or sage powder in bottles on the spice rack. As you transition from this strong, rather bitter-tasting powder to fresh or dried leaves, you will discover a new dimension of sage and wonder how you ever got along without it. The value of this culinary and medicinal herb was illustrated when the Dutch traded sage to the Chinese—receiving in return three times as much non-sage tea. A final interesting fact: the English once traded sage for opium!

Growing

Sage, *Salvia officinalis*, is a hardy perennial in Zone 4. It likes an alkaline, well drained sunny spot in a garden, and a light porous medium soil. It grows to be 18 to 24 inches high, and that wide as well. Leaves are gray, pebbly, and lanceolate. Because of its color, sage makes a nice accent plant in landscaping. Sage is a tough perennial and will overwinter beautifully outdoors in the ground. Mulch around sage plants with straw. Mulch prevents the splashing of mud and dirt on the leaves, which have a hairy, pebbled surface and are hard to clean.

Sage comes in several varieties. Golden, purple, and tricolored sage have delightful colors and make beautiful landscaping plants. They are wonderful as garnishes for sagey dishes, and they make nice foliage additions to bouquets. However, these three colored sages have not been reliably hardy in our area.

Propagating

Sage grows easily from seed, which is readily available, and makes a nice 4-inch potted plant 10 weeks after seeding. We use a 72-cell tray and plant several seeds per cell. We cover the seed with vermiculite, cover the tray with clear plastic, and set the bottom temperature to 70°F. Germination should start in about 9 days and be completed in fifteen. Lovely purple and blue blossoms will appear in the second year. Sage will live many years in one spot, but with age, the stems become woody and scraggly. So, we change locations and plant new plants every 3 years. We also prune our plants yearly.

Harvesting

You can cut off leaves anytime after the plant has become established. It actually does better the more it is cut back, but always be sure to leave at least a quarter of the leaves to regenerate. Sage is usually harvested from May through October. (The Greeks were even more specific and state that sage should be harvested May 1 before sunrise!)

Preserving

Dry sage by hanging bunches of whole leaves upside down in a well ventilated, dark place. The air should not be warmer than 76°F. The volatile material will vaporize. When the sage is dry, store it in a dark, air-tight container. The flavor is better if you store the leaves whole. To use them, crush or rub them. Also store sage by making oils, butters, and sage vinegar, which is tasty with mild vegetables.

Cooking

The flavor of sage is grand. Authors of old herbals stress that the medicinal properties are most efficacious in May. An English proverb states, "He that would live for age, Must eat sage in May."

The robust taste of sage can be the single flavoring for just about any vegetable. It is also good with pork, fish, game, legumes, cheese, eggs, and butter.

You won't learn this in most cookbooks, but sage makes an outstanding tea that has many medicinal properties. For example, strong sage tea is a mouthwash that treats colds and soothes sore gums. It has anesthetizing and healing qualities that we find superior to commercial remedies. It's not surprising that an old Italian proverb says, "Why should a man die whilst sage grows in his garden?"

To use fresh sage for frying or stir-frying, brown the leaves in butter or oil until crisp (sometimes with garlic and onions). Remove the leaves and fry the food. When broiling or roasting, lay sage leaves on the food and remove them when serving. Use fresh sage as a garnish. The whole leaf blends nicely with steamed vegetables. For egg dishes, sauces, cheeses, and dressing, chop fresh sage and add to the dish.

Dried sage also works with the above methods. Rub dried leaves in your hands. A fluffy, powder forms. Remove the stems and the result is called rubbed sage.

Sage's flavor stands up to long cooking periods and high heat. However, it imparts a richer flavor if added to dishes the last few minutes of cooking.

❧Herbed Rice❧

Makes 7 servings

1 shallot or small onion
3 tablespoons butter
1 cup rice
2 cups chicken stock or bouillon
1 bay leaf (preferably fresh)
12 sage leaves, chopped
12 sprigs thyme, chopped
3 sprigs each tarragon and marjoram, chopped
salt and pepper

Chop shallot or onion and cook until soft in melted butter in heavy saucepan. Add rice and stir to coat. Add bay leaf and chicken stock or bouillon, and bring to a boil. Cover saucepan, reduce heat to simmer, and cook 20 minutes. Remove bay leaf and add chopped herbs. Salt and pepper and serve.

❧Sage Butter❧

½ cup butter
1 clove garlic, crushed
10 to 15 sage leaves
1 teaspoon lemon juice
salt and pepper to taste

Cut butter in small pieces. Chop sage leaves in small pieces. Pound together with a mortar and pestle or use a blender or food processor. Blend in garlic and lemon juice.

Serve with pork chops, venison steaks, fried eggs, fried potatoes, steamed carrots, cauliflower, and beans. Use purple, tricolor, or a mixture to add interest.

❧Sage Dressing❧

8 cups dried bread crumbs
½ cup butter
1 cup warm water, bouillon, chicken or vegetable stock
1 cup chopped onion
1 cup chopped celery
3 tablespoons chopped fresh sage leaves or 1 tablespoon dried
    sage leaves
salt and pepper to taste

Melt butter in saucepan. Add onions and celery and saute. When onions become translucent, add liquid. Mix bread crumbs, sage, salt and pepper. Add sauteed mixture and liquid. Taste for seasoning and adjust as necessary. The mixture should be moist enough so a ball of it holds its shape. Makes enough dressing to stuff a large chicken or a small turkey.

❧Applesauce with Sage❧

6 cooking apples
2 teaspoons sugar
1 tablespoon chopped sage, about 6 leaves
water

Peel and core apples. Cut into slices and lace in saucepan with enough water to cover the bottom of pan. Stew gently until soft. Add sugar and chopped sage. Serve with roast pork or duck.

❧Sage Fritters❧

1 cup all-purpose flour
2½ teaspoons baking powder
1 teaspoon salt
½ teaspoon pepper
1 egg
½ cup milk
oil for frying
50 sage leaves (approximately)

Batter: Sift flour, baking powder, salt, and pepper into mixing bowl. Combine eggs and milk. Mix liquid ingredients into dry ingredients until smooth.

Heat the oil to 375° in frying pan. Coat each leaf with batter and place in hot oil. Fry, turning once, until golden brown. Drain on paper towels and serve immediately.

❧Sage Soup❧

Serves 4 to 6

¼ cup cooking oil
2 medium onions, chopped
3 stalks celery, chopped and diced
2 pounds potatoes, peeled
5 cups chicken stock or bouillon
10 fresh sage leaves
salt and pepper
⅔ cup milk

Saute onions and celery about 6 minutes. Add potatoes, stock, and 4 chopped sage leaves. Cover and cook until potatoes are tender (25 to 30 minutes). Salt and pepper to taste. Add milk. Serve hot in bowls. Add a fresh sage leaf for garnish on each bowl.

❧Herbed Pheasant❧

MARINADE:
1 bay leaf
3 sprigs marjoram
6 sprigs thyme
7 leaves sage
3 sprigs summer savory
6 leaves basil
2/3 cup dry white wine

ROASTING INGREDIENTS:
3 tablespoons cooking oil
1¼ cups chicken stock or bouillon
3 sprigs each thyme and summer savory
3 stalks lovage
7 leaves sage
Salt and pepper to taste
Parsley for garnish

Mix chopped marinade herbs with wine, and pour over pheasant. Refrigerate 12 to 24 hours, basting with marinade several times.

Remove pheasant from marinade and place in roaster or flame-proof covered casserole. Add oil, and brown on all sides. Combine stock, or bouillon, and marinade. Add salt and pepper. Heat and pour over the browned bird. Place herb sprigs and leaves around the bird. Cover the pan and place in a preheated (325°) oven for about 2 hours, or until bird is tender. Slice and serve. Garnish with parsley.

❧ *Onions in Sage Sauce* ❧

1 pound boiling onions
2 tablespoons butter
2 tablespoons all-purpose flour
1 cup milk
6 chopped sage leaves
1 tablespoon chopped parsley
salt and pepper to taste

Steam onions 20 to 30 minutes until tender. While onions are cooking, melt butter in a saucepan over low heat and mix in flour until smooth. Add milk. Increase heat to medium and stir mixture until thickened. Add chopped herbs and onions. Season to taste. Serve warm.

THYME
Thymus vulgaris

CHAPTER 12

Thyme

Common thyme, *Thymus vulgaris*, which is the thyme most people use for seasoning, has a pungent taste and what some would call a medicinal aroma. A similar aroma comes from cough drops, syrups, and antiseptic preparations with a plant constituent in the ingredients. However, we prefer to think of thyme's smell as herbal, and we find its pungent, peppery flavor appealing. Apparently, common thyme's name is too common because it has several other names, including garden thyme, English thyme, French thyme, summer thyme, and winter thyme.

Caraway thyme, *thymus barons*, is a prime flavoring for Baron of Beef, a round roast beef preparation of some repute, and is an excellent addition to coleslaw. It is a trailing plant and thus makes an excellent hanging basket. The leaves are dark green and lance-shaped; the flowers are rose colored.

Lemon thyme, *Thymus x citrodorus*, is a highly desirable cooking herb. It grows upright to eight inches. It has a distinctive lemon flavor and aroma.

Growing

Common thyme, a hardy perennial of moderate life in the North, is easy to grow from seed. It has whitish pink flowers and grows upright to a height of 18", spreading a couple of feet in a season. Because the seed is very small, plant it in a seed bed or container, and transplant it after the plant has gained some size.

It has a slow growth rate, so plant it in a weed-free place. It likes full sun and thrives in rich, well drained soil. It is also a heavy feeder, taxing our light, sandy soil. It tends to die out in the center and it seems to affect the soil so it should be divided and moved at least every 3 years. This thyme should also be mulched for overwintering in northern climates.

All of the above thymes like dry, well-drained soils with a high ph (7.5 to 8). We add five pounds wood ash to a 25-foot row before planting. The wood ash alkalizes the soil while providing healthful organic nutrients.

Thyme makes an attractive potted plant, and such low growing thymes as caraway thyme make nice hanging baskets. However, as house plants, thyme will not produce enough to be a good source of out-of-season fresh herbs. But the leaves can supplement your dried thyme supply and can also be used for garnishes.

Propagating

Common thyme can be grown from either seed or cuttings. Seeds germinate in 4 to 5 days. We plant them in cell trays, several seeds to a cell, for transplanting. We do not cover the seed, but we do cover the tray with clear plastic and have the bottom heat at 70°F. It grows slowly at first but makes a saleable 4-inch plant in 12 weeks.

Caraway Thyme roots easily from cuttings, and since it roots wherever it contacts the soil, layering it is easy. In the North, it should be mulched for overwintering. Lemon Thyme is propagated from stem cuttings, using the same method as for French tarragon, it roots fairly easily in about 2 weeks.

In our experience neither caraway thyme nor lemon thyme has produced viable seed, so we propagate them from stem cuttings or by layering. Both send down roots from their leaf nodes. Cut them from their parent plants once roots form. To help thyme plants overwinter, allow them to go into winter with some good growth.

Harvesting

Harvest thyme for cooking whenever the plant is actively growing. Cut off stems as needed. Strip the leaves from the stem, which is often tough and inedible. It is good to shape and renew the plants several times a year. When you do this, also plan a major harvest for drying. We do two large harvests in June and late August. For large harvests, take it just as it starts to flower, but always leave one-third of the plant.

Preserving

Drying is the best way to preserve thyme, which is one herb that maintains its flavor and aroma when dried. We cut thyme in small bunches, each bunch the diameter of a nickel and 6 inches long. We bind the bunches with rubber bands and place them upside down in a dry, dark, airy place. We hang a few bunches in our kitchen for appearance, but for full flavor you should store dried thyme in an airtight container in a dark, cool environment. You can also freeze thyme or use it to flavor vinegars, oils, and butters.

Cooking

Thyme is used frequently in herb cooking, and a rule of thumb may well be, *"When in doubt, use thyme."* Thyme is used in combination with many other seasonings, and it often mimics their flavor. Thyme is used in meats, fish, soups, stews, and herbal sauces. It is also used with, or in place of, rosemary, sage, oregano, or savory.

Substitute caraway thyme for caraway seeds in coleslaw and other dishes. Other species that are used culinarily are *Thymus serpyllum* and *Thymus pulegioides,* which both have the flavor of common thyme. Thyme is also good in the recipe for Grilled Summer Vegetables with Tangy Lemon Butter, on page 132. You will find a use for either fresh or dried thyme in many recipes. It is all over the culinary scene. Just let your imagination go!

❦ Grilled Herb Beef Patty ❦

1 serving

¼ pound extra lean ground beef
⅛ teaspoon each coarse ground pepper, dried rosemary, and
    dried thyme leaves
1 slice onion (¼-inch thick)
1 teaspoon Dijon-style mustard

Form ground beef into a patty ½-inch thick. Combine pepper, rosemary, and thyme. Gently press into both sides of patty. Place patty on grill over ash-covered coals or on a rack in a broiler pan. Grill or broil 8 to 10 minutes, turning once. Brush both sides of onion slice with oil. Place the onion on the grill or broiler just after turning the patty. Turn the onion once, and brush it with mustard. Serve beef patty with grilled onion. *(Contributed by Beef Industry Council.)*

❦ Herb and Garlic Dipping Sauce ❦

2 cups beef stock or beef bouillon
2 tablespoons chopped basil
2 tablespoons chopped marjoram leaves
2 cloves garlic, crushed
1 tablespoon each chopped thyme, rosemary, and oregano leaves

Combine ingredients. Warm over low heat, but do not boil. Serve like au jus, as a dip for sliced roast beef or roast beef sandwiches.

❧ Herb Blend for Vegetables, ❧ Meat, and Poultry

½ cup marjoram, dried
¼ cup sage, dried
¼ cup thyme, dried
¼ cup rosemary, dried
¼ cup oregano, dried

Combine ingredients thoroughly. Store in a small air-tight container. *(Contributed by the Minnesota Grown Program.)*

❧ Fresh Creamed Corn ❧

Serves 4 to 6

2 tablespoons butter
½ cup chopped onion
½ cup each chopped red and green pepper
1 clove garlic, minced
3 cups fresh corn kernels
¼ cup chopped green onion
1 cup half-and-half
2 tablespoons chopped fresh basil
2 teaspoons chopped fresh thyme
salt and pepper to taste
1 tablespoon flour
4 slices bacon, cooked, drained, and crumbled
1 tablespoon fresh parsley

Melt butter in large skillet. Saute onion, peppers, and garlic until tender (about 3 minutes). Add corn, green onion, half-and-half, basil, and thyme. Simmer, uncovered, 5 minutes or until corn is tender. Season to taste with salt and pepper. Sprinkle flour over corn. Cook and stir until thickened (about 2 minutes). Sprinkle with bacon and parsley. Serve immediately.

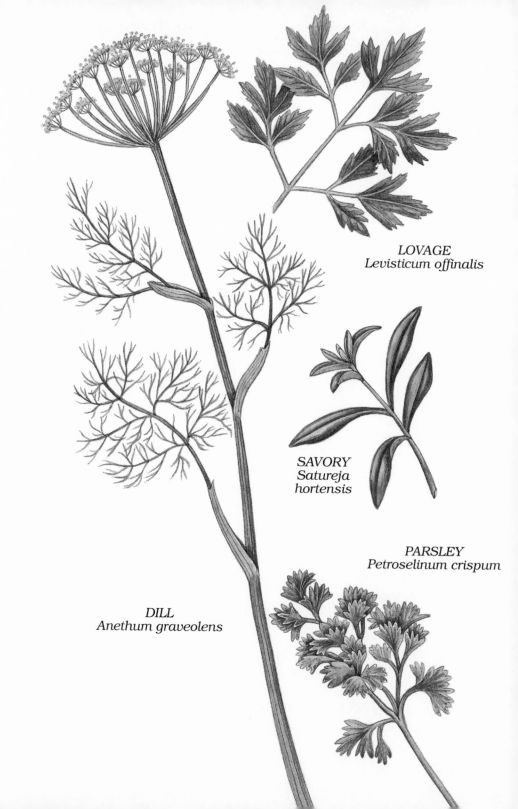

LOVAGE
Levisticum offinalis

SAVORY
*Satureja
hortensis*

PARSLEY
Petroselinum crispum

DILL
Anethum graveolens

CHAPTER 13

Other Culinary Herbs

Bay Laurel

Bay laurel, *Laurus nobilis*, is the same herb from which the phrase "laurels of honor" originates. In Classic times, victors were honored with laurel wreaths, the fuzzy stuff pictured on heads in old Greek and Roman statuary. In its Mediterranean home, bay laurel grows to be 50 feet tall.

Although it stretches the botanical description of "herbacious" (it is an evergreen tree in its natural environment), it too is an example of the adaptability of living things. It makes a wonderful culinary pot plant as it is very attractive with its dark glossy, spear-shaped leaves. It can be trained or pruned to a standard but since it is extremely slow growing it will take a long time. (A standard is an herb, grown with an erect tree-like stem, not dwarfed by grafting and not trained on a wall or trellis.)

We start our bay laurel plants from seed and plan for a long-term project. We use a peat light soil mix with 72°F bottom heat. Because the seeds are large (big as plum seeds), we bury them ½ inch in the medium. It took 40 days for the first seed to germinate, and our most recent one came up after 6 months! Be sure to use fresh seed, since old seed loses its viability.

Since most bay laurel plants on the market are produced by cuttings, there is not much information on growing them from seed. To start them from cuttings, take the cutting from the terminal growth, that is from branches that are still growing. Cut off about four inches of the stem or branch, remove the lower leaves, and stick the cut stem into a sterile sand or soil mix. Keep the medium moist and warm (70 to 80°F.) Put your cuttings in full light but out of direct sunlight, and cover then with plastic to retain moisture. The plastic cover should be vented (lifted) daily and removed when growth begins.

Cuttings need from 60 to 180 days to root. Move the rooted cutting to a pot no larger than 4-inches, as the bay laurel plant seems to prefer a root-bound condition. If you buy a rooted cutting or a seedling bay plant and want it to produce lots of leaves for your culinary creations, we suggest that you keep it root-bound. Move it to a larger pot only when it will no longer stay moist or it has stopped growing.

As a rule of thumb, the 4-inch pot should be adequate the first year; repot the second year into a 6-inch pot and the third year into a 10-inch pot. The fourth year, we use a 5-gallon container. After that we just change the soil each year and prune our bay tree. In the summer we place the plant in a sheltered sunny spot.

We overwinter our bay tree in a sunny, cool environment indoors, misting it twice a week during the heating season. It likes a moist soil so we don't let it get too dry before watering. However, we make sure that both the container and the soil are well-drained.

We fertilize twice a month in the late spring and early summer, and once a month during the rest of the year. We use a fertilizer with a complete formula plus micronutrient at recommended strength.

Diseases and pests are usually not a problem for bay plants. When we have noticed some scale, we use light horticultural oils with insecticidal soap.

Leaves may be picked at any time, as long as you allow at least one-third of the leaves to remain on the plant. If you start with a seedling, do not harvest for the first year or two.

Bay leaves can be used fresh or dried. The uses for the leaves are many. They make your stews flavorful, are essential for *Bouquet garni*, and are very good in soups, sauces, and casseroles.

Bay has a strong flavor, and the leaves give up their flavor slowly, so this is one herb you can cook a long time. Just about any hearty soup recipe calls for a bay leaf. Most cooks add a bay leaf to beef stew, which has a long cooking time. We use bay in any marinade that is used with beef. It also gives a touch of piney flavor to homemade bouillon. Other slow cooking dishes that take on a new dimension with a bay leaf are custards and rice pudding.

Some cooks use bay leaves as an insect repellent in rice or grain caches, placing a few leaves in the storage container. This practice also gives the grain a subtle flavor.

A few cautions with bay. It is a strong herb, so use one leaf to about two pounds of meat, or about two quarts of liquid. Remove bay leaves from the dish before serving. Fresh leaves cook up soft, but dried leaves remain tough. You can also powder the leaves. Powder gives a stronger flavor and should be added at the end of your cooking rather than at the beginning.

Chervil

As a fresh herb chervil is seldom found in American markets and, since it doesn't retain its flavor when dried, you will have to grow your own if you want to use it. It is a lovely plant, frilly with dainty leaves and small white flowers. Chervil looks a bit like parsley, and is often used in place of parsley. Chervil has a sweet flavor that is faintly like tarragon or anise.

We recommend growing chervil from seed, planting it where you want it to grow, since it sometimes bolts when transplanted. The seed usually germinates in a week, so keep it weed-free. Chervil grows well in cool, moist weather, and it doesn't mind a little shade. Since it will bolt and go to seed in the dog days of summer, you will have to make serial plantings (along with your dill, cilantro, and arugula). If you plant chervil in a somewhat shady spot, it maintains its leafy growth instead of going to flower.

Chervil Soup

Serves 4

1 bunch green onions, chopped (7 to 10)
¾ pounds potatoes
¼ cup butter
1½ cups chopped chervil
3¾ cups hot chicken bouillon
¼ cup lemon juice
1 tablespoon vinegar
salt and pepper to taste
1 egg yolk
¼ cup sour cream, sweetened with 1 tablespoon maple syrup or honey

Wash and chop green onion. Peel and slice potatoes. Melt butter in saucepan over low heat and simmer onions 3 to 4 minutes. Add potatoes and chervil and cook another 2 minutes. Pour hot bouillon over vegetables. Cover and simmer another 25 minutes, until potatoes are soft. Cool slightly, then puree them in a blender. Strain through a sieve until smooth. Return to a clean pan and reheat just to boiling, but do not boil. Add lemon juice and vinegar. Salt and pepper to taste. Beat egg yolks in a small bowl. Stir 3 tablespoons of the hot soup into the egg yolk. Whisk soup and egg mixture into the soup. Heat through. Pour into cups. Garnish with the sweetened sour cream and a leaf of chervil.

Sherried Wild Rice Soup

Fresh herbs and sherry add special flavor to this rich, creamy wild rice soup.

¼ cup margarine or butter
½ cup finely chopped onion
½ cup thinly sliced celery
½ pound sliced mushrooms
¼ cup all purpose flour

3 cups chicken broth
2 cups cooked wild rice
1 tablespoon chopped fresh chervil
¼ teaspoon salt
¼ teaspoon white pepper
1 cup half-and-half
⅓ cup dry sherry or additional broth
chopped fresh parsley for garnish

Melt margarine in large pan over medium heat. Stir in onion and celery. Cook 5 minutes until tender, stirring occasionally. Stir in mushrooms. Cook 2 minutes or until slightly tender. Stir in flour until well blended. Stir and cook 1 minute. Gradually stir in broth. Cook, stirring constantly, until mixture boils and is thick. Stir in rice, chervil, salt, and pepper. Reduce heat to low. Stir in cream and sherry. Cook, stirring constantly until heated thoroughly. Serve in soup bowls. Garnish with fresh parsley. *(Contributed by Minnesota Paddy Wild Rice Council.)*

Dill

The seed head of dill, *Anethum graveolens,* is used to give dill pickles their unique flavor. We use fresh chopped dill leaves in salads and on cottage cheese. The chopped leaves are also good mixed with melted butter, salt, and pepper then poured on new potatoes, chopped cabbage, baby carrots, green beans, cauliflower, or summer squash. You can use dill to flavor fish, lamb, pork, poultry, cheese, and eggs. It can be found in many eastern European and Scandinavian recipes.

Dill is a hardy, fast growing annual that is easy to grow. The trick to growing dill is to plant it early in the season so the soil stays moist during germination. If you plant in hot, dry weather, keep the soil surface moist so the seed does not dry out.

You can either seed it directly into your garden or transplant it. For transplanting, we seed six seeds per cell in the 72-cell tray. Germination is generally good with dill, so we have a large number of plants in each cell. We do not thin them, but transplant the cluster of plants as a clump from each cell. Dill needs light to germinate, so do not cover the seed with soil or mix when you plant it. Cover the tray with clear plastic put it under light with a bottom heat of 70 to 75°F. You'll see sprouts in 5 to 7 days. Let them grow in the cell tray for another 3 weeks before transplanting into the garden.

For direct seeding, either plant the seeds in your garden before the fall freeze-up, or as soon as the soil is ready for planting in the spring. Then make successive plantings until August to get a full season's production, as the plant dies after it sets seed. Dill grows in either drilled or wide rows. However, young dill is not a competitor with fast growing annual weeds. Dill can be closely planted if you are going to use it as dillweed. If you want the dill to mature and have flower heads for pickles, space the plants so there are 3 to 4 per foot. If you plant in the fall, wait until it is cold enough so that it will not germinate.

The primary method to save dill for out-of-season use is harvesting the seeds. Leaves and stems lose most of their flavor in drying, and freezing discolors leaves, You can make vinegars, oils, and butters using dill, but seeds meet most seasoning needs. You can grind seeds and use them as you would the whole dill seed.

Harvest dill weed when it is about 6 inches tall by pulling the young plants up by the roots, or cutting them at ground level. Clean it by running water over the roots and feathery tops, or by plunging it into a container of clean water.

Shake the bunch and blot it with a towel before chopping it for use. You can either chop it with a sharp knife, or snip it with a scissors for sprinkling on your entree.

To harvest seed head dill, it is important to watch for the change in the color of the seeds around the outside of the seedhead (umbrel) from green to brown. We cut the head with about 6 inches of stem.

If we are saving seed, we place the heads in a bunch inside of a brown paper bag, and hang it to dry. For use in dill pickles, the head is also harvested when the seeds begin to go from green to brown.

❧Dill Sauce❧

½ cup mayonnaise
¼ cup fresh dill, chopped
1 tablespoon lemon juice or herb vinegar
salt and pepper to taste

Blend all ingredients and refrigerate a few hours to meld the flavors. This sauce is good, hot or cold, on poached or broiled fish.

Fennel

There are a variety of fennels, but they all are anise flavored with varying degrees of sweetness. This distinct taste is what cooks and chefs are looking for. They use the seeds as teas and to flavor shellfish, fish, and fish sauces. Seeds are also added to bread, spaghetti sauce, pickles, pastries, cookies, rolls, and cheese spread.

Bronze fennel, *Foeniculum vulgare var. rubrum*, and sweet fennel, *Foeniculum vulgare var. azoricum*, are equal in every respect except color. Bronze fennel has a copper color that is a nice addition to the landscape, while sweet fennel is a beautiful pale green. The seeds, stems, and leaves of these plants may be used. *Foeniculum*, or sweet fennel, is a perennial but is not winter-hardy in the North.

Florence fennel is an annual. If planted in the North about July 1, it forms a bulb and won't bolt to seed. Florence fennel needs short days or cool nights in order to bulb. If you plant it in early spring, it will most likely bolt. Once it has bolted, it will not produce a bulb.

We understand there are new varieties of fennel you can grow anytime in the growing season. Supposedly, they produce a bulbous stem without bolting, but we have not experimented with them.

We start two or three seeds in each cell and cover the seed lightly with the soil mix, cover the tray with plastic, and put it under the lights with 70°F bottom heat. The seeds germinate in about 6 days. You can plant it outside when the soil thaws, or you can transplant it into the ground in early May. We give each single fennel plant one foot in the row, and our rows are one foot apart. It is hardy to light frost. It generally will go to seed, so you can use the leaves and seeds for flavorings.

Start cutting the ferny leaves when the plant is established. Take the plant's outside branches, always leaving the growing point where new leaves are coming out of the stem. The leaves are nice in salads or as a garnish on fish dishes. If you grow the plant for seed, do not remove any growth because this decreases seed production. The seeds, which resemble a dill head, are usually ready to harvest around the end of August. Cut off the entire head, put it in a large paper bag, and allow it to dry in the bag in a dry, warm environment.

Fennel and Tomatoes
4 Servings

4 fennel bulbs
¼ cup cooking oil
1 pound tomatoes (2 to 3 fair sized tomatoes)
fennel leaves
salt and pepper to taste

Cut fennel bulbs in thin vertical slices. In a heavy pan simmer slices in oil until almost soft. Add sliced tomatoes and continue cooking gently for 5 minutes. Sprinkle chopped fennel leaves over tomatoes and fennel bulbs, and turn out into a serving dish to cool. Serve cold, but do not chill in the refrigerator; this diminishes the flavor.

Garlic

Garlic, the *Allium* perhaps best known for its medicinal and culinary attributes, should be a main herb in your garden. The variety that grows best in cold climates is Rocambole.

Plant garlic in the fall 6 to 8 weeks before the ground freezes. Once the ground freezes, mulch the garlic until about April 1. Garlic likes regular moisture and a well drained fertile soil in full sun, but it doesn't like to compete with weeds. Rocambole sends up a seed stalk in early summer. Most growers break it off as soon as the flower head starts to enlarge, supposedly allowing the garlic cloves to grow larger. Garlic is ready to harvest when the leaves begin to dry out. You can preserve it by drying or mixing it with oil and freezing. See chapter 2 for more information on preserving techniques.

A bonus to growing your own garlic is using the greens (tops) of the plant, which have a pleasant garlic taste. Use the greens like green onions or chives; add them to egg dishes, stir-frys, salads, and many other dishes.

Garlic is used the world over. Most Oriental and Latino dishes contain garlic, as do many southern and eastern European recipes. It is a main ingredient in pesto (see page 44 for the recipe). It is increasingly popular with Americans, who are appreciating garlic's flavor and aroma. But be advised that flavor and aroma vary; much depends on the variety, where it was grown, the age of the bulb, and the storage conditions. (This advice applies to other herbs as well.) How you cook garlic also affects taste and aroma. Fried, steamed, baked, and poached garlic have different flavors. Garlic's odor bothers some people, but you can alleviate the problem by adding an equal amount of fresh parsley to garlic recipes.

❧Flavored Garlic Vinegar❧

Garlic makes an excellent flavored vinegar by itself or with other herbs.

1 pint cider, rice or white wine vinegar
3 garlic cloves, peeled and chopped
3 fresh hot peppers, chopped
2 cups (loosely filled) of any of these herbs: tarragon, thyme,
    sage, marjoram, dill, chives or mint

Mix garlic, peppers, and herbs in a scalded jar or bottle. Fill with vinegar, making sure you cover herb mixture. Top with a non-metallic cap or cork, and place in cool, dark place. (A non-metallic lid is necessary since vinegar reacts with metal lids.) The vinegar is ready in 2 to 3 days. You can add more vinegar to the jar as you use it, or when the vinegar has the flavor you like, strain out herbs, garlic, and peppers. Use the vinegar as you would plain vinegar—for marinating vegetables and meats, as a substitute for lemon juice, in salad dressings, or to add flavor (a teaspoonful at a time) to steamed or braised vegetables.

❧Chicken Garlic with New Potatoes❧

4 servings

This recipe uses garlic almost as a vegetable. It gives the cloves a sweet nutty taste, and seasons the chicken and potatoes in a robust Middle European way.

4 to 5 tablespoons olive oil
4 to 5 whole heads of garlic, peeled* (35 to 40 large cloves)
2 tablespoons fresh basil, chopped
2 tablespoons fresh oregano sprigs
4 skinned, boneless chicken breasts
1 dozen small early potatoes (skin on)
fresh oregano and basil to taste.

Pour olive oil in a baking pan large enough to hold the chicken and potatoes. Place peeled garlic cloves in olive oil and stir to coat cloves. Place in a 350° oven for 12 minutes. While garlic bakes, clean and dry chicken. Scrub potatoes and halve them. Remove garlic from oven and add chicken and potatoes. Baste chicken and potatoes with olive oil from the pan. Add oregano and basil. Cover pan. Return pan to oven for about 60 minutes, or until potatoes are cooked. Garlic and chicken will be ready at the same time. Divide the dish among four serving plates. Garnish with fresh basil and oregano leaves or green garlic tops.

*If you don't like peeling garlic, place cloves in the olive oil (skins still on) in a roasting pan. Roast about 15 minutes at 350°. Remove from oven. Cool so you can handle them. Squeeze each clove with your fingers, and skins will slide off.

Horseradish

Horseradish, *Armoracia rusticana*, is a highly acclaimed condiment. Some people feel that eating roast beef without grated horseradish, or at least a horseradish sauce, is like eating sweet corn without butter, salt, or pepper. It has a sharp, mustardy taste, and its volatile oils will make your eyes water and your nose run—even more so than strong onions.

Horseradish is a hardy perennial grown from root cuttings. It may set viable seed, but its seeds are seldom used for propagation. Horseradish is difficult to eradicate once established because the plant can regenerate from a small piece of the root. The root is grown commercially in a rather complicated ritual. A 6- to 9-inch piece of root is planted horizontally in the soil in early spring. In early July the root is partially lifted and trimmed of rootlets to make a smooth, large root for harvest in the fall.

We plant the root piece vertically, with the top just below the soil's surface. We let it to grow until late October, when we harvest the whole root. We do not leave any rootlets in the ground unless we want to increase our plantings.

We prepare horseradish on the back porch rather than in the house; the fumes of the chopped herb make us weep and weep. We wash and peel the roots and rootlets, then we shred or grind them. To each cup of ground horseradish we add ¼ cup water and 2 tablespoons of vinegar. We blend the mixture to be stored in the refrigerator for several months. Used it as is, like mustard or catsup, or mix with white sauce, catsup, or other sauces to add a tangy flavor.

We mix 2 or 3 tablespoons of prepared horseradish with 1 cup of catsup to make a dip for cocktail shrimp. Another good dip is mayonnaise mixed with prepared horseradish. This is a particularly good sandwich spread with roast beef or poultry.

Horseradish is a terrific accent in the following delicious tidbit:

❧Cucumber-Shrimp Bites❧

2 medium cucumbers
salt
1 package (8 ounces) cream cheese, softened
1 can (4¼ ounces) small shrimp, rinsed and drained
2 tablespoons each chili sauce and finely chopped red pepper
1½ teaspoons prepared horseradish
½ teaspoon dried basil
¼ teaspoon seasoned salt
⅛ teaspoon pepper

Peel cucumbers and trim ends. Cut each horizontally in half. Scoop out seeds. Sprinkle centers with salt. Turn over and place on paper toweling. Drain at least 30 minutes. Meanwhile, combine remaining ingredients in small mixer bowl. Beat on high speed until well blended. Fill cucumbers with shrimp mixture. Wrap filled cucumbers in plastic wrap. Chill 1 to 2 hours. To serve, cut cucumbers into ¼-inch thick slices. Garnish as desired. *(Contributed by the American Dairy Association.)*

Lovage

Lovage, *Levisticum officinale*, is a hardy perennial that is especially tasty in soups, salads,and casseroles. The entire plant is useful—leaves, stems, roots, and seeds—and all parts have a flavor of strong, raw celery. We say "LOVEage" but the French say something like "LOVASZH". Lovage is a tall, leafy plant. Leaf stalks are 2½ feet tall, and the flower stalk grows as tall as 6 feet. It looks like celery, except the stems are round. The blooms in July are a dill-like yellow umbrel.

This herb is easy to grow. It does well in full sun or in shade. You can divide lovage in the spring or you can grow it from seed. It is important to use fresh seed as it does not retain its vitality for very long. If you grow your own seed, it will be ready to plant as soon as it dries on the stalk in late July. You can also make root divisions in the spring. Lovage is one of the first perennials to poke its leaves out of the ground in the spring, so you can add it to your spring salads and tonics.

Lovage makes a nice 4-inch pot plant in about 7 weeks, and it should be transplanted to the garden soon after that, 10 weeks at the latest. We plant several seeds into each cell of wetted Cornell soil mix and cover it with medium-sized horticultural vermiculite. We cover the tray with plastic, give it bottom heat of 70°F, and expect the seeds to germinate in 8 to 10 days. We then thin one plant per cell. Lovage will reseed itself in the garden so if you want to keep it contained and you do not use the seed, remove the seed head before it matures.

Lovage makes a great straw for sipping Bloody Marys. The celery flavor adds to the drink as you sip through the stem. The stem is closed at the nodes, so cut between the nodes or puncture them. You can also garnish the drink with lovage leaves.

Lovage seeds are flavorful, too, green or dried. Dried seeds hold their flavor well for winter use. The seed head should begin turning brown before you harvest it. Cut the entire head, tie several together at the stems, and hang them in a paper bag. Close the bag and when seeds have dried, shake them into the bag and blow off the chaff. Place the seeds in air-tight containers and store them in a dark, cool, dry environment. Lovage makes a good vegetable stock you can use as a base for soups and sauces.

Potato Soup

Serves 4

1 large onion, diced
1 cup celery chopped
2 tablespoons butter
5 medium-sized potatoes, diced
¼ cup lovage stems and leaves, chopped
Salt and pepper to taste
Water to cover
1½ cups milk

Saute onion and celery in butter over low heat until onions are clear. Add potatoes and lovage. Cover with water and bring to a boil. Cover pan and simmer until potatoes are soft. Add milk and continue simmering until soup is reheated. Salt and pepper to taste. Garnish with fresh lovage leaves and serve.

Lovage Stock

Saute 1 cup chopped onions in 2 tablespoons butter. (If you want a brown stock, let onions caramelize. If you want a clear stock, do not let them brown.) Add ½ teaspoon each black pepper, cayenne pepper, and salt. Combine onions with the following ingredients in a saucepan:

1 good sized carrot
1 piece of daikon radish, same size as carrot (a turnip or a bunch of red radishes can be used instead of the daikon)
1 head shredded lettuce (we like Romaine, but any kind will do)
1 cup lovage leaves and stems, chopped
water to cover

Bring to a boil; cover, and let simmer about 1 hour. Add a *bouquet garni* of 4 sprigs parsley, 1 bay leaf, and 3 sprigs fresh thyme, tied together. Simmer another 20 to 30 minutes. Remove *bouquet garni*. Stock is ready to use. Makes about 1 quart.

Parsley

It is a pity that most people throw away the parsley garnish on their plates. We think parsley should be on everyone's windowsill so it is readily available to be used in scrambled eggs, fried and boiled potatoes, soups, salads, sandwiches, and as a bright green garnish in the middle of the winter. Its high chlorophyll content makes parsley *"Mother Nature's breath fresher,"* so if you want to be kissable, eat parsley! (But be careful, as you may have green leaves stuck between your teeth.)

Parsley is often used as a garnish, but use it in in larger amounts in the herbal dishes we suggest. As mentioned in our garlic section, you can combine equal parts of parsley with garlic to modify garlic's odor and taste. Parsley is also high in vitamin C and iron.

Parsley is easy to grow. It is biennial, and it likes a moist, cool situation. It will live in full sun or partial shade. It will tolerate some frost so you can plant it early and harvest it late. We grow two types of parsley: Italian (flat leafed) and curled (crispy.) They both grow well and they each produce about the same amount of leaves. Some of our customers say that the flat leafed has more flavor while others vote for the curly. We use them both liberally.

If you are planting from seed, be sure to use fresh seed; seeds do not stay viable for long. We always buy new parsley seed every year, since the seed will lose its viability if held longer. We start our parsley in a 72-cell tray, several seeds to a cell. We cover the seeds with vermiculite, cover the tray with clear plastic and place the tray under lights with a bottom heat of 70°F. In 8 to 10 days, parsley is popping up all over. The parsley will be ready to pot up into a 4-inch pot or to move outside in about 5 weeks.

We have heard that transplanting parsley is not the best method for propagation, but we have had poor luck with seeding it directly into the garden so we have been transplanting it now for 10 years with good results. However, transplanted parsley is not as drought resistant because the taproot of the transplanted plant doesn't go as deep into the soil as if it were direct-seeded. We solve that problem with irrigation.

Parsley planted outside takes up to a month to germinate, depending on the temperature, so mark your planting site and keep the weeds down. Parsley flourishes in partial shade to full sun in a fertile, moist soil. If you are growing it in sandy soil, amend the soil with compost or peat moss.

Growing parsley indoors requires some attention because the plant cannot dry out, and also requires fertilizer to produce usable greens.

Harvest parsley by pulling one stem at a time from the outside of the plant. If you need a large amount, cut the entire plant off at ground level and bunch it with a rubber band. The plant will grow back to a harvestable size in 4 to 5 weeks. We get 4 to 5 harvests from an early planting. Sometimes we side-dress it with an organic fertilizer after the second cutting if it seems to be slowing down.

Parsley does not dry well. Preservation options are to freeze it in oil (see page 20), freeze it (unblanched) in a plastic bag, or grow a pot of it on your window sill.

Parsley is generally used in *fines herbes* with chives, tarragon, and chervil. Mix equal amounts of each herb, chopped fine, and add at the last minute of cooking. Parsley is also a filler when making pesto or herb oils and herb butters. It dilutes the flavor of stronger herbs like rosemary, sage, basil, and oregano.

❧Parsley Stuffing❧

1 good sized onion, chopped
¼ cup butter
6 cups dried bread crumbs
½ to 1 cup water or other liquid, such as chicken bouillon to
    moisten the stuffing
½ cup chopped parsley
salt and pepper to taste

Follow instructions for sage dressing found on page 139. Makes enough stuffing for one large chicken.

❊Parsley Soup❊
Serves 6 to 8

1 large bunch of parsley
1 pound potatoes
½ head lettuce (2 cups, chopped)
1 large onion, chopped
2½ quarts water
salt and pepper to taste

Chop parsley, potatoes, lettuce, and onions. Place all ingredients in a large kettle with the water. Add salt and pepper, and bring to a boil. Reduce heat and simmer, covered, until potatoes are cooked, 45 to 60 minutes. Garnish with fresh parsley and serve hot. Soup can also be sieved or pureed and served with a dollop of sour cream.

Rucola, Rocket, or Arugula

The same great salad herb is known by these three names. It is a hardy annual that you can seed directly in your garden. Rocket has a nutty, sharp flavor that seems to ebb and flow by the day. When rocket is small and young, its flavor is mild and it has the texture of young Bibb lettuce. As the plant ages, the taste becomes sharper, somewhat like radish or mustard, but it retains the texture of tender lettuce. While rocket is mainly a salad ingredient, we understand that in Italy it is used in many cooked dishes. Steamed rocket sounds good, but we have not tried it yet.

Rocket is a hardy annual in the North. You can plant it when you can work the ground in early spring, and because it germinates and grows fast, it is excellent to grow from seed. You can also transplant it, something we do for weed control. We do multiple plantings in the season and recommend the same. After rocket flowers, it becomes tough and strong tasting. Still, many people find it tasty at this stage.

For transplanting, we use the 72-cell tray, 4 to 5 seeds per cell. We cover the seed with vermiculite, cover the tray with clear plastic, and set the bottom heat to 75°F. In 3 days we will usually see germination. The seedling will be ready to transplant in 3 weeks, and ready to eat or sell in 3 more weeks. We plant every 2 weeks from early May through August, and we really crowd them.

If we direct-seed rocket in the garden, we drill 6 to 10 seeds per foot. We transplant clumps of three plants every three inches. The only problem we have had with this crop is early infestation of flea beetles. The plants usually outgrow the damage, but harvest is delayed.

For salads, cut off individual leaves or cut the plant off above the crown, it will regrow. If you are going to market it, we recommend digging the whole plant and bunching it with the roots attached. It will remain turgid (unwilted) longer with roots. Putting it in water also helps. We harvest the whole plant because of our serial plantings. We have been told you can keep the same plant growing all season if you prevent it from flowering.

We have never tried to preserve rocket for later use, although it does seem you could make a pesto or sauce from rocket and freeze it.

❧ Rocket (Arugula), Daikon, ❧ and Cucumber Salad

⅓ cup distilled vinegar or rice wine vinegar
2 tablespoons sugar
¼ pound daikon radish
1 large cucumber, peeled
½ teaspoon salt
¼ pound arugula
1 tablespoon sunflower seeds

Combine vinegar and sugar. Shake or stir until sugar is dissolved. The mixture can be slightly heated. Cut daikon into thin strips, about 2 inches long. Peel the cucumber, remove seeds, and cut into thin strips, about 2 inches long. Combine daikon and cucumber in a sieve set over a bowl. Toss with salt. Allow to drain at least 20 minutes. Squeeze out as much moisture as possible.

Line the serving plate with rocket. Combine daikon, cucumber, and vinegar-sugar dressing, and mix. Place on the arugula. Sprinkle with sunflower seeds and serve.

Savory

Summer savory, *Satureja hortensis*, is a fast growing annual. Winter savory, *Satureja montana*, is a slow growing perennial. Both have a similar hot and pungent taste. Some say they are an excellent replacement for pepper. We use them interchangeably and think their flavor goes well with practically all meat and bean dishes, and with sauces over pasta and vegetables. We strip and chop fresh leaves and add them at the last minute to soups, sauces, stews, and hot dishes. Savory is also good in poultry and pork stuffings, alone or with sage or rosemary. Finally, savory combines nicely with parsley and oregano.

Summer savory is usable in all stages of growth. A tender annual that grows quickly from seed to its full and useful size, savory likes full sun and a well-drained, fertile soil. We grow it in a flower box on the back deck so it is easily available.

Plant several of the small seeds into each cell of a 72-cell tray. Do not cover the seed, but cover the tray with clear plastic and place under the lights with a bottom temperature of 70°F. You will see germination in about 5 days. The seedlings will be ready to transplant up or out in the garden in 3 weeks and make a saleable 4-inch pot plant in another 4 weeks.

Savory can be harvested ruthlessly as it continues to grow new leaves and stems from its old stems. It makes a nice pot plant and grows well in the house, but it needs a lot of light. In the garden, plant it in clumps where its small lilac-pink flowers put on a pretty show. The foliage turns light purple in the late summer, to a nice effect.

Winter savory grows much more slowly than summer savory. It is hardy in Zone 3, and it likes a dry, well drained position. We start it from seed in February, and it generally reaches a height of about 8 to 10 inches by the time it freezes in the fall. Winter savory is an attractive plant and works well as a house plant for overwintering. You will not get much growth out of it inside, but it can be trimmed for seasoning.

Shallot

The shallot, another *Allium*, is in the realm of herb cookery because it has a unique blend of mild onion flavor and aroma. Use shallots in sauces, casseroles, and as a seasoning on vegetables. Shallots may be finely chopped or cut into rings and added to vegetable salads for a taste treat. You can also use them in salad dressings and for replacing onion or garlic. You can saute shallots and simmer them in butter over low heat. Try topping steaks or chops with them; we add chopped sweet basil or tarragon to the topping. In making omelets or scrambled eggs, add about 1 tablespoon of finely chopped shallots per egg. Other fresh herbs combine nicely with the shallots in egg dishes.

We plant shallots as soon as the ground thaws in spring. They require a fertile, sunny area, well drained and weed-free. Grow shallots from individual cloves, like garlic.

When leaves start to die down in mid-July, the shallots are ready to harvest. Dig the whole plant. It will have multiplied from the single clove you planted to 10 or 12 cloves. Dry shallots in a cool, dry place out of the sun. Store in a mesh bag in a cool dry place (50 to 55°F). They will probably keep until planting time in April or May.

❧Shallot White Sauce❧

Good with steamed asparagus, beans, carrots, broccoli, cauliflower,
or any other vegetable that takes a white sauce.

2 tablespoons butter
2 tablespoons flour
1 cup milk
8 to 10 shallots, finely chopped
salt and pepper to taste

Melt butter in a saucepan over low heat. Add flour to melted butter
and mix. Cook mixture 2 minutes and add milk. Raise heat to medium-
high and stir until mixture boils. Remove from heat and stir in chopped
shallots. Salt and pepper to taste.

❧Shallot Sauce❧

Good over steamed vegetables and on broiled fish, steak, or chops.
Garnish with tarragon sprigs.

1 cup beef bouillon
½ cup tarragon vinegar
8 to 10 finely chopped shallots
2 tablespoons flour (approximately)
2 tablespoons fresh tarragon, chopped

Mix vinegar with beef bouillon. Add shallots and simmer over low
heat until shallots are tender, 15 to 20 minutes. Thicken with flour. Add
chopped tarragon.

Sorrel

You can cut sorrel, *Rumex acetosa*, into small narrow strips and use
it as a sour accent in salads or as a garnish on other vegetables. The
leaves have a lemon flavor.

To make a puree of sorrel, shred 1 cup of the leaves and add to 1 tablespoon of butter. Heat and stir until leaves dissolve into a puree. The sorrel will be reduced to less than ¼ cup. Multiply this formula to meet your needs. Add sorrel puree to vegetable puree such as winter squash, rutabagas, parsnips, and carrots. Sorrel puree also enlivens a number of egg dishes.

❧Sorrel Soup❧

1 quart vegetable stock (or enough vegetable or chicken bouillon
    to make a quart of liquid)
1 cup sorrel leaves, finely chopped
1 cup lettuce leaves, finely chopped
salt and pepper to taste

Bring stock or bouillon to a boil and add leaves of sorrel and lettuce. Lower heat and simmer about 10 minutes. Salt and pepper to taste and serve hot.

Sweet Marjoram

Sweet marjoram, *Origanum marjorana*, is similar in flavor and aroma to oregano, and works well in almost any recipe that calls for oregano. Marjoram, however, has a milder, sweeter taste and smell than oregano. It is good with beef, lamb, poultry, fish, and vegetables. You can use it in stews, sauces, dressing, soups, and stuffings. Marjoram is also a major flavoring in sausage. Sometimes for breakfast we sprinkle a handful of chopped fresh marjoram stems and leaves over eggs and potatoes as they fry. This lets us skip the sausage and still have its flavor and aroma!

Sweet marjoram is a tender perennial. However, it grows well from seed, so we grow it as an annual. The seed is small, so we start it in a seed tray and transplant it to the field. Marjoram grows well in a sunny, well drained soil and reaches a height of about 12 inches. It is a rather decorative gray-green plant that produces hop-like flower heads.

Plant in cell trays as you do other annuals. Leave the seeds uncovered, but cover the tray with clear plastic and set the bottom heat to 75°F. You will see green in 4 to 5 days. Do not thin, but plant them up in clumps and transplant into your garden the same way.

We harvest marjoram to dry or sell when the flowers form. You can harvest the entire plant, or just the leaves and stems, at any time. Leave at least half of the leaves to regenerate the plant. Regrowth of the new plant is from the roots, but growth is slow. Therefore, expect only one cutting per season. You will get three to four harvests per year from late spring-seeded transplants.

Marjoram, which dries well, can be used fresh or dried in recipes. However, fresh marjoram has quite a different taste than the dried. To dry it hang bunches in an airy, dry, dark, and warm environment. You can also preserve marjoram in vinegars, oils, and butters.

Minestrone with Marjoram

3 tablespoons olive oil
3 garlic cloves, chopped
2 large onions, chopped
2 quarts chicken or vegetable stock
2 large carrots, cubed
1 large potato, cubed
5 or 6 medium tomatoes, skinned and seeded
1 medium zucchini, cubed
¼ pound green beans, cut into 1-inch lengths
1 pound greens (spinach, chard, Chinese cabbage, etc.), shredded
1 16-ounce can kidney or navy beans or 2 cups cooked beans
2 tbsp. fresh marjoram
1 cup dried elbow macaroni

Saute onions and garlic in olive oil in a soup pot over medium heat until onions are clear, about 3 to 4 minutes. Add stock, carrots, potatoes, and tomatoes. Continue cooking over medium heat until potatoes are cooked, 15 to 20 minutes. Add zucchini, both kinds of beans, greens, pasta, and marjoram. Salt and pepper to taste. Return soup to simmer for another 10 minutes. Serve with Parmesan cheese sprinkled on top and with crackers.

BASIL
Ocimum basilicum

MINT
Mentha

Herbal Teas

There are a number of reasons to drink herbal teas. Most herb teas have carminative properties, which is to say they aid in digestion, and many also supply vitamins, minerals, and other constituents that can help maintain wellness. In addition, the act of gathering herbs is a visual and olfactory stimulant, shifting your mind from the freeway and high tech office, and awakening a sense of your ancient, or archetypal, past. The result is a feeling of comfort and well-being.

There are almost as many herbal tea recipes as there are tea brewers. You can make a tea easily with a crushed handful of fresh herbs and an 8-ounce cup of boiling water. If the herbs are dried and crushed, we use 1 to 2 teaspoons of the herb per cup of water. We dry our herbs on the stem and store them in plastic bags. We then put these bags inside brown paper sacks in a cool, dry cupboard. When we want tea, we remove the dried herbs from storage, strip leaves from stems, and crush them in the process. We place them in a large paper bag and measure the material for tea. This way, we can blend and mix as many different combinations as we like.

You can use a teapot, or any covered container, for making teas from leaves. Place tea material in the container, pour boiling water over it, cover, and let it steep for 3 to 5 minutes before serving.

If you are using roots, bark, seeds, or fruit for tea, then simmering is best. Put the material in a saucepan filled with the amount of boiling water you desire. Cover the pan, and reduce the heat. Simmer 10 to 20 minutes. Some roots, seeds, and barks commonly used for tea are licorice root, comfrey root, valerian root, ginger root, willow bark, cinnamon bark, cherry bark, cramp bark, rose hips, fennel seeds, dill seeds, sweet cicely seeds, and angelica seeds.

Whether you steep or simmer your teas, the final step before serving is to strain it. Tea bags, balls, and nets take care of the straining for you. The herb material is placed in one bag, for example, which is suspended in a cup or teapot of boiling water. The device usually has a string or handle, so you can move it back and forth.

Some nutrients in the herbal material are contained in volatile oils. To prevent them from escaping, cover the pot or cup when you steep or simmer your tea. Any condensation on the bottom of the cover can be added to your pot or cup.

The following herbs make good single ingredient teas. As you make these teas for medicinal purposes or just plain enjoyment, remember to sip it slowly and allow yourself to inhale its essence.

Basil

The many varieties make for interesting tea material. In addition to lemon and licorice basil, try sweet basil, cinnamon basil, the small leafed basils, or Thai holy basil. The two purple basils, purple ruffles and dark opal, add a pleasing visual touch to your teas, especially a frosted glass of iced tea garnished with purple basil.

Chamomile

The little daisy flowers of German chamomile, *Matricaria recutita*, make an apple-scented tea reputed to be a mild sedative, digestive aid, and an antiseptic. It is also used to relieve menstruation pains and premenstrual migraine headaches. The tea has a pleasing taste and is probably the most popular herbal tea.

German chamomile is a 23-inch tall annual with apple-scented, fern-like leaves and a 1-inch daisy-like flower used in hair rinses. It is a fun herb because the bloom appears, disappears, and then reappears a short time later with another bloom all through the summer. Chamomile likes a sunny spot and a light, well-drained soil. It will tolerate some shade and many soil types. Here in central Minnesota it blooms June through August and readily reseeds itself. Its seeds are very tiny (300,000 per ounce) so we seed it into cell trays. Germination is generally below 50 percent so we put a pinch in each cell, cover the tray with clear plastic and put it under lights with bottom heat of 70°F. We usually see green in 7 to 10 days. After danger of frost has passed, we plant the seedlings outside.

English or Roman chamomile (*Chamaemelium nobile*) is a perennial creeping plant with fern-like leaves and a small white daisy-like flower that appears in September. We harvest and dry the blooms just as they open and make tea with them. Roman chamomile is best grown from seed. Cultural practices are the same as for the annual chamomile.

Cold Relief Tea

When coming down with a cold, we combine equal parts of *Marrubium vulgare* (white horehound) with one of the *Monardas*, either *Monarda fistulosa* (wild bergamot), *M. didyma* (bee balm), or *M. punctata* (horsemint.) This medicinal tea needs a honey sweetener, as it is very bitter without one.

Garden Sage

(Salvia officinalis)

When used internally, sage has a reputation for reducing bodily secretions, such as sweat, saliva, lactation, and mucous in the sinuses. Sage is also used as a gargle for a sore throat, and as an anti-bacterial mouthwash. See chapter 11 for growing instructions.

Lemon Balm

(Melissa officinalis)

Lemon balm is used as a garnish, as a medicinal tea, and as a substitute for lemon flavor. As the name implies, this herb has a lemon flavor and scent. As a tea it is reputed to relieve stress and act as a mild sedative. Taken at bedtime, it ensures a good night's sleep. Don't be afraid to double the dose, either fresh or dried, from the standard tea measurements; it is quite mild in action and taste.

Melissa officinalis is a hardy perennial, 18" tall. It takes full sun to partial shade. You can plant the seed, or propagate by division or cutting. We usually plant from seed since it makes a nice 4-inch pot plant in about 6 weeks. We seed in the 72-cell tray, sprinkling several of the 50,000 per ounce seeds into each cell of wetted Cornell peat lie mix. We don't cover the seed, but we cover one tray with clear plastic and put it under growing lights with a bottom heat of 70°F. The seeds will germinate in about 7 days, and will be ready for a 4-inch pot in 3 weeks.

To harvest, the plants may be cut off at ground level any time after the plant is established in your garden.

Lemon Flavored Herbs

Many herbs are lemon flavored. They all make excellent teas, alone and with other herbs. The most popular is the aforementioned lemon balm. Others are lemon basil, lemon grass, lemon mint (*Monard citridora*), lemon thyme, and lemon verbena. A plant that similar to lemon balm is dragonhead, also known as Turkish Melissa (*Dracocephalum moldavica*).

Licorice or Anise-flavored Herbs

Some of these excellent herbs are sweet, and are used as sweeteners in tea combinations. Licorice root, anise hyssop, and sweet cicely are all strong sweeteners. French tarragon (see chapter 7), licorice basil (page 37), and mint marigold make nice anise-flavored teas. Fennel seeds have long been used for mild sweet teas that parents sometimes give to infants for upset stomachs (it also works for adults).

Orange Mint

Orange mint has a bergamot flavor we like. *Monard didyma* (bee balm) also duplicates this flavor. It is sometimes called Oswego tea after the eastern US Native American group that introduced it to the rest of the world. See chapter 8, the mint chapter, for more information.

Peppermint

A good carminative tea for after a large meal, peppermint helps to dispel digestive gas and prevent its formation. Herbalists claim that a cup of this lovely tea has many benefits. It is thought to be anti-spasmodic, anti-inflammatory, a liver stimulant, an anesthetic to the skin, and a remedy to increase concentration. See chapter 8, the mint chapter, for more information.

Purple Passion Tea

A particular tea combination we find comforting is 1 part purple ruffles basil, 1 part lemon grass, and 2 parts peppermint. It is good hot or cold, and a mint sprig makes a nice garnish.

Rosemary

A tea made from it is reputed to be a cure for weak minds. 'Nuff said. See chapter 10, the rosemary chapter, for more information.

Spearmint

Hot or cold, this is another excellent mint tea. Spearmint mixes well with other herbs, so feel free to experiment!

The following herbs make fine teas, by themselves or in combinations. This list is not all inclusive. A good herbal will explain the chemistry and use of each plant.

Other combinations you may wish to try:
- spearmint, lemon balm, sweet basil
- chamomile and peppermint
- chamomile and lemon balm
- scented geranium, lemon grass, and sage
- elderberry, rose hips, and peppermint
- catnip, fennel seed, and lemon basil
- spearmint, anise hyssop, and purple ruffles basil.

The list could go on and on. Just determine what you like and try it. We understand that when the Celestial Seasonings owners first started their business, they had a tea containing 36 different herbs they had gathered, dried, and blended. Combinations are limitless. If you use teas as remedies or for medicinal purposes, consult an herbalist. Also, be sure you know what you are gathering. You will not go wrong with culinary herbs, but do your homework if you venture into others. Good brewing!

DAY LILY
Hermerocallis fulva

JOHNY JUMP UP
Viola kitaibeliana

Edible Flowers

Edible flowers include most culinary herbs, several bedding plants, and numerous perennials. We caution you to make sure you know your plants. Also be sure that they have not been sprayed with any herbicide, fungicide, or pesticide. We have eaten all the flowers described here and have suffered no ill effects. Another caution: Don't overdo it. Moderation is the key.

Using edible flowers as edible garnishes is exciting. The flowers stimulate the appetite and make a dish an artistic creation and a gourmand's delight.

We usually pick the flowers 2 to 3 hours before dinner is to be served. We find this to be a nice, relaxing thing to do before the busy moments of final food preparation.

We gently run water over them, place them on a fluffy towel to drip for a minute or two, and place them, gently, in a plastic bag in the refrigerator until ½ hour before serving time. These chilled flowers are placed on the food (nasturtiums on salad, borage on tomatoes, Johnny jump ups on anything) and can be eaten in their entirety.

Anise Hyssop

A favorite of ours is anise hyssop (*Agastache foeniculum.*) It grows tall and lanky, but the flower is a raceme about 2 to 4 inches long. It is purple with a sweet anise smell and flavor. This flower is an excellent addition to sweet fruit salads, sweet drinks, and desserts.

Basils

Basil flowers are pretty and excellent tasting. Cinnamon, licorice, purple ruffles, Thai basil, and dark opal basil all have colored flower stems that make great garnishes. Cinnamon basil flower stems make a good decoration for puddings and fruit salads. The flower stems are too tough to eat, but the flower petals are quite sweet and tasty. Sprinkle sweet basil blossoms on tomato slices. See chapter 4, the basil chapter, for more information.

Bergamot Flowers

Bergamot flowers, *Monarda didyma*, range from white to red to purple. The flavor is the source of the name bergamot. The taste is like Earl Grey tea, which is flavored by a citrus plant called bergamot orange. You can strip bergamot's stiff stem of the leaves, and use the shaggy head as a stir stick for fruity drinks. Remove individual flowers from the calyx and use them for color in salads or other dishes.

Borage

The borage plant's small blue or pink flowers make an excellent addition to sliced cucumbers or tomatoes. An easy annual to grow, borage, (pronounced "boridj"), is adaptable to most soils. *Borage officinalis* grows fast and easy from seed planted directly in your garden, and it will reward you with lovely blue star-shaped flowers to garnish drinks and salads. If you want to start borage early, you can transplant it, but it is a big, fast grower so only 5 weeks from seedling to transplanting is about right. It will reach 2 to 3 feet high and 18 inches wide. For the best view of the flowers, plant it on a terrace or wall so the blooms will hang down in a graceful cataract of color.

Grasp the blossom between the index finger and thumb of one hand. With the other hand grasp the calyx (the green part of the plant that holds the flower) and separate the two. Place the blossom on the cucumber or tomato, or on salads, desserts, pastries, and in drinks. Blossoms also can be crystallized or candied (see recipe on page 190).

Day Lily

The day lily is another spectacular flower, large and multi-colored, that will command "oohs" and "ahs." Picture a dish of Bibb lettuce, sliced red onions, cucumber slices, arugula leaves, sliced green olives, vinaigrette dressing, and crumbled feta cheese. Garnish with a yellow day lily surrounded by red-orange nasturtium blossoms. Spectacular! Your guests will want to save it.

Marigolds

Try using two marigold plants, sweet marigold (*Tagetes lucida*) and lemon gem (*Tagetes tenuifolia*), as edible garnishes. Sweet marigold has a sweet licorice flavor. The leaves and yellow flowers accent sweet dishes and drinks. Lemon gem marigolds have a lemon flavor, and the possibilities for its use are limitless.

Nasturtium

Impress your guests with the decorative and tasty nasturtium blossoms and leaves. They will spice up and shape up any green or fruit salad. To produce flowers, nasturtiums like it cool, dry, and sunny, but the plant will continue growing and producing leaves during hot weather also. There are both dwarf and climbing nasturtiums. A fence or some structure to climb is needed for the latter. The dwarf variety makes nice hanging baskets, window boxes and edging.

Nasturtiums can be direct-seeded into your garden or into a container. We plant them into 4-packs to sell as bedding plants, but we don't expect them to be content very long in a small container. Figure on 5 weeks from the time you seed them to planting out in a small container like a 4-pack.

Add it to any salad or dish that can use fresh radish or watercress. Use nasturtium's leaves and flowers as a garnish with salads, meat dishes, desserts, and drinks. Once you see how nasturtiums dress up your culinary creations and what a zing the flowers and leaves add to a dish, you are going to be a nasturtium grower. However, they are not hardy, so wait until the danger of frost is past to plant. Our only other advice on nasturtiums is don't over-fertilize them.

You can pick leaves and flowers at any time. Always leave at least half the leaves for regrowth. Nasturtium seeds are also delicious when they are green.

Scented Geraniums

Scented geraniums come in many different shapes and fragrances. Their flowers, while not as profuse as garden geraniums, are nonetheless worth your efforts. They range in color from white to purple to red with many shades between. Some bi-colored, spotted, or striped. Some of the scents are rose, peppermint, coconut, apple, apricot, orange, lemon, ginger, Old Spice, and nutmeg, to mention a few. They also make delightful garden plants. There are as many different plant forms as there are scents, and if you plant them along a walk, they will please both your eyes and your nose as you move among them.

Scented geraniums can be grown from seed, but since we have not been able to find any seed on the market, we have planted seed from our own apple and nutmeg geraniums and have good success. We plant them in a Cornell Peat-Lite mix and treat them just like the other annual herbs. We propagate most of the geraniums that we sell using cuttings. We take cuttings 12 weeks before we will need finished 4-inch pot plants. We like a cutting that is about three inches long. We take it from the stock plant and place it in a cool, dark place for 2 days to allow a callus on the cut to be formed. (The callus is the tough covering that forms over the cut surface, from the which the roots will grow). Then we place the callused cutting into a 50-cell tray, water them in and place the tray under a white plastic tent with a bottom heat of 75°F. After 2 to 4 weeks the cuttings will have formed enough roots to be transplanted into 6-inch pots. It takes about 15 weeks for most of the geraniums to flower. Some of them flower almost continuously; others for 4 to 5 weeks and others flower during the winter.

Scented geraniums are tender perennials in Minnesota, but they make a delightful, fragrant house plant. Instead of letting old Jack Frost do them in, pot them in the fall and give them a well-lighted spot in your home. They will reward you with a pleasant aroma whenever you touch them.

If you are wintering them in your home, remember to keep them a little root bound and clean off any dead foliage. Scented geraniums differ in size and in flowering habits. You may enjoy starting a collection. They like it a little cooler than most of us keep our houses (but they get along at 70°F also.) Go easy on the fertilizer. Try one-half as much as on other plants. It takes a long time for geraniums to blossom, so do not pick off the growing points. Some people swear geraniums do better if they are ignored.

While we use scented geraniums mainly for their form and scent, they may also be used for teas, garnishes, and flavoring as all of them are supposed to be edible. The essential oil of the rose geranium is used in perfumes and cosmetics. Other geraniums are used in potpourri, sachets, and Tussie Mussies, an herbal bouquet popular in Elizabethan times to mask street smells. The dried crushed leaves of any of the geraniums make a good room air fresher.

Others

Other flowers: Onion chives and garlic chives produce delightful blossoms that give taste and color to salads and other dishes. The small blue rosemary flowers that adorn the plant in September and October have a sweet, piney flavor. The raceme of the lavender plant makes for a sweet-smelling garnish. They would be difficult to eat, but the individual blossoms are edible. The purple blossoms of garden sage, *Salvia officinalis*, of purple and tricolored sage, and of other *salvias* (e.g. red

189

blossoms of pineapple sage) make excellent garnishes. The leaves of purple, tricolor, golden, and garden sage dress up a dish with a sage flavor. They can also turn a breakfast of eggs, sausage, and hash browns into real spa cuisine. Mint flowers can embellish your masterpieces, as can thymes and scented geraniums. Thymes and mints blossom at midsummer. Pansies and Johnny jump-ups are glorious additions to dishes, but they don't offer much in taste. Pansies cover countless color combinations, while the small jump-ups tend toward blues and yellows.

There are other edible flowers, some that we've tried (like roses as well as squash, apple, and plum blossoms) and many we have not. Experiment with those we have mentioned. You will be rewarded many times over.

❧Sugared Flower Petals❧

borage blossoms, rose petals, mint leaves
egg white, slightly beaten
superfine granulated sugar

Dip blossoms, petals. or leaves into the egg white, or paint the egg white on them with a small paint brush. Cover blossoms with the sugar, gently sprinkling it on. Place blossoms on an ungreased cookie sheet. Place in oven on a very low setting, leaving the door ajar. Let blossoms dry 4 to 6 hours. Served immediately, or you can keep them in an airtight container. Store in a dry place.

A second way to crystallize flower petals or leaves: Bring to boil a mixture of 1 pound sugar and 1 cup water. Heat until mixture reaches 240°. Make sure leaves and flowers are dry. Drop them into the sugar mixture, a small handful at a time. Lift them out immediately with a slotted spoon. Place on aluminum foil or a cookie sheet. Place in oven at lowest setting to dry. Turn once during the drying period.

The main use for these lovely squared petals is as a decoration on cakes. They can also be placed on sweet desserts, such as puddings. Rosebuds with a little coconut on vanilla pudding makes a plain dessert into something special.

Recipe Index

Index